Sails for Cruising
Trim to Perfection

Sails for Cruising
Trim to Perfection

Mark Chisnell

fernhurst BOOKS

Copyright © Fernhurst Books 1998

First published 1998 by Fernhurst Books,
Duke's Path, High Street, Arundel, West Sussex,
BN18 9AJ, UK.
Tel: 01903 882277 Fax: 01903 882715

Write, phone or fax the publisher for a free,
full-colour brochure.

Printed and bound in Great Britain

British Library Cataloguing in Publication Data:
A catalogue record for this book is available
from the British Library.

ISBN 1 898660 46 8

Acknowledgements
Many thanks to all the staff at Hyde Sails who
helped with the preparation of this book, but in
particular to Christian Brewer, Richard Franks,
Dave Hall and Mike Lennon. Thanks also to Nick
Beloe and Jeremy `Pasty' Vigus for helping to
sail the boats; Dan Belton at Ancasta and Clem
Noel for loaning the two yachts; Rick Tomlinson
for his patience through the photo shoot and, of
course, to Tim Davison, Calvin Evans and
Edward Hyde for their support.

Cover design by C E Marketing.

All photography by Rick Tomlinson.

Design and DTP by Creative Byte.

Edited by Tim Davison.

Printed by Hillman Printers, Frome.

Contents

Foreword

It's long been our philosophy here at Hyde that cruising sails should be more than just triangles with holes in the corners. We're firm believers in the idea that cruising can be both more enjoyable and safer with well designed and well built sails. But of course, that means the sailors should know how to set, trim and care for them. And, traditionally, sail trim has perhaps been a little frowned upon among the cruising fraternity – as the unhealthy competitive preoccupation of the racers! But if you pay good money for something you want to be able to use it properly and, just as importantly, you want it to last. Which is why we are delighted to be involved with this book, perhaps the first one on sails and sail trim to be devoted purely to the needs of the cruising sailor. We're particularly pleased that Mark Chisnell has written it – as he's been associated with Hyde Sails, as a sailor and a scribe, since his school days in dinghies. We're sure that this book will help you achieve safer and more comfortable cruising in a clear and precise fashion. And of course, it might get you where you want to go a little quicker too!

Good reading and enjoyable sailing.

Edward Hyde

1 Aerofoils and Isaac Newton

An aerofoil being used as a spoiler on a racing car.

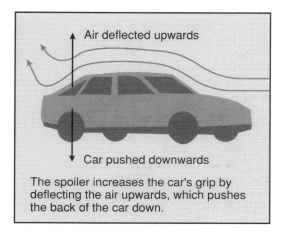

The spoiler increases the car's grip by deflecting the air upwards, which pushes the back of the car down.

A sail is just one of the many aerofoils around us. From the spoilers on performance cars to wind generators, aerofoils are a common feature in our lives. The aquatic equivalent is the hydrofoil, of which the rudder and keel are examples. Both aero- and hydrofoils are useful because they generate a force from the flow of fluid (be it air or water) around them. How they do this can be explained in terms of Isaac Newton's Third Law of Motion.

Newton's Third Law

Newton's Third Law of Motion states that t*o every action there is an equal and opposite reaction.*

So if I drive my spoiler laden car into a brick wall (action), the brick wall will collapse and fly backwards and my car will stop (reaction). There is a little more in the detail, and engineers earn a living calculating where every last joule of energy disappeared in friction, heat, momentum of the bricks and so forth. But the principle is simple enough. So how does it apply to a foil?

Spoilers

Many modern cars have spoilers. But what do they do? The air comes streaming over the windscreen and roof, and onto the boot where it hits the spoiler. The spoiler deflects the air upwards. And according to Newton's Third Law, if the spoiler deflects the air upwards, then the spoiler itself (and the back of the car it's attached to) must be pushed downwards - into the road. Which is why spoilers are there, to push the back of the car down and increase the grip the tyres have on the road.

Flat plates as foils

We can see from the action of the spoiler on a car that even something as simple as a flat plate will act as a foil. If you put your hand out of the window of a moving car (making sure you're not going to knock it into something!) and put it flat to the wind, you'll find it is pushed backwards. Now tilt it to 45 degrees to the wind with the front edge lower and you will find that it is pushed downwards as well as back. The action is exactly the same as on the spoiler at the back

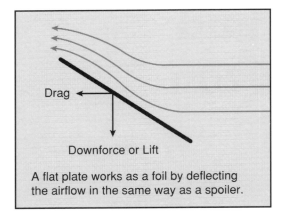

A flat plate works as a foil by deflecting the airflow in the same way as a spoiler.

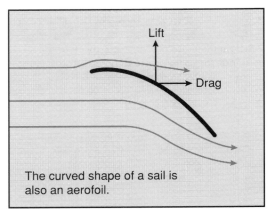

The curved shape of a sail is also an aerofoil.

of the car. The flat plate of your hand deflects the air upwards, and is itself deflected down and back.

It's important to notice that the flat plate is pushed downwards and backwards. Nothing comes for free, and the cost of the spoiler achieving more grip for the tyres when you are going round corners is that it slows up the car when it's going in a straight line. Which is why you hear so much these days about tuning the wings in Formula One. The spoilers are aerofoils, or wings, and getting the right balance between the downforce and the drag is critical to the car's performance.

Lift and drag

We can separate the force generated by the flat plate into two components, one pushing the plate downwards, the other pushing it backwards. We'll call these lift and drag. The science of aero- and hydrodynamics is all about the lift and drag generated by any given shape of foil and its angle to the flow of water or air. Generally, lift is the one we want to maximise and drag is the one we want to minimise, through the efficient operation of the foil.

Curved foils rather than flat plates

Clearly flat plates don't make very efficient foils, otherwise you would see them on Boeing 747's (although they will let a plane fly, albeit a paper one). In fact a flat plate will only generate lift

when it is at an angle to the wind. In contrast, the curved shape of a 747 wing is efficient enough to generate lift in level flight with the airflow parallel to the foil. It does this in part by being an asymmetric shape, which is a quality that a sail shares. This allows sails to work at a very fine angle of attack. Unfortunately, because it's a soft foil it cannot work in a direct airflow, because the sail would be unable to hold its shape without some angle to the flow.

While curved foils do work better than flat plates, they also come in different shapes and sizes for different jobs. Compare the wings on a light propeller aircraft to those on the 747 or a fighter jet. Or the spoiler on the back of a family saloon to that on a Formula One race car. The reasons for all this are deeper into aerodynamic theory than we have the space or the need to

The trimtab on a 6-Metre racing yacht allows the keel to take up an asymmetrical shape and so act as a foil even without leeway.

explore here. We only need to know that some shapes and angles of attack to the flow are more efficient than others. There are more practical methods for us than research into aerodynamics to find out which ones.

Sails as aerofoils

We started this book by stating that a sail is an aerofoil, and we can now see how it acts as a foil by deflecting the wind. Good sail shape and sail trim is all about deflecting the wind efficiently, to get the maximum lift and the minimum drag from the sail. We will do that by a combination of adjusting the shape of the sail and varying its angle to the wind.

Keels and rudders as hydrofoils

We also stated at the beginning that keels and rudders are hydrofoils. They act by deflecting the water in the same way that sails deflect the wind. Keels and yachts don't travel through the water in a straight line, they drift or `crab' sideways. This crabbing through the water is called leeway, and all yachts make leeway, except when they are sailing dead downwind. As we can see, leeway allows the keel to deflect the water flow and generate lift, in exactly the same way as the sails do. It would be possible to build a keel that would not require any leeway, that would generate lift with the water flowing directly onto it, like an aeroplane wing. But this requires an asymmetric shape, and that's expensive to construct for a sailboat, which has to sail on both tacks. But it is done in some racing boats, through a device called a trim tab. But for cruising boats leeway remains both an inconvenience, allowing you to drift away from your destination, and essential to your sailing - because without it keels couldn't generate lift, and without that sailboats wouldn't sail in any direction other than downwind. That's because sailing is the product of the balance of the forces generated by the sails, keel, rudder and hull.

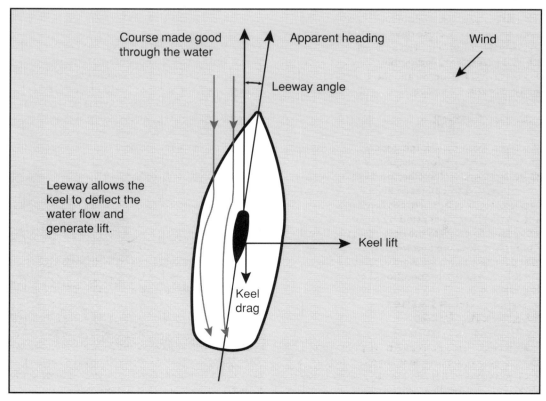

Course made good through the water

Apparent heading

Wind

Leeway angle

Leeway allows the keel to deflect the water flow and generate lift.

Keel lift

Keel drag

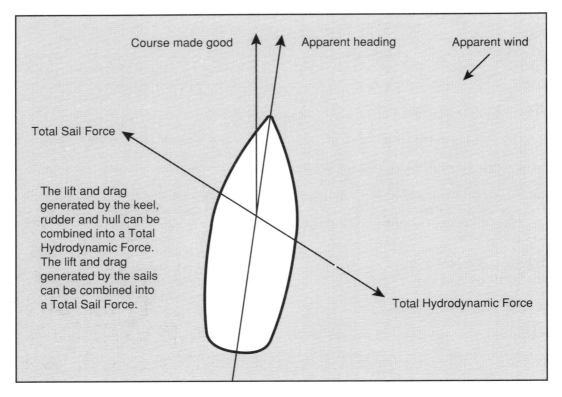

A Balance of forces

The aerofoil forces generated by the sails and the hydrodynamic forces generated by the keel, rudder and (to a limited extent) the hull, can all be combined. The total forces are called the sail force and the hydrodynamic force. It can also be established that the total sail force acts through a point in the sailplan (called the centre of effort), and the hydrodynamic force acts through a point in the keel (called the centre of lateral resistance) - much as the weight of a pencil acts through a single point when balanced on your finger. And balance is the key; for the boat to maintain its course, sailing in a straight line, these total forces must balance. There are important things that we can learn about sails and sail trim from this balance.

Weather helm and lee helm

We have seen that the total sail force acts through the centre of effort and the total hydrodynamic force acts through the centre of lateral resistance. When these two are in line above each other the boat will sail in a straight line by itself; there is no resulting force that is trying to turn the boat. But if someone now lets the headsail flap its contribution to the centre of effort will be lost, and the centre of effort will move aft, behind the centre of lateral resistance (page 12). This creates a turning moment that is trying to point the boat into the wind. This is called weather helm, and you'll know when you've got it, because if you let the wheel or tiller go, the boat will automatically point up into the wind.

The opposite occurs if you let the mainsail flap or flog. In this case the centre of effort will move forward, ahead of the centre of lateral resistance, and create a turning force that is trying to push the bow away from the wind. This is called lee helm (page 13). Both of these forces can usually be resisted with the rudder. And that is the most important point - the sails affect the load on the helm. The way you trim and set the sails can either help or hinder you in steering

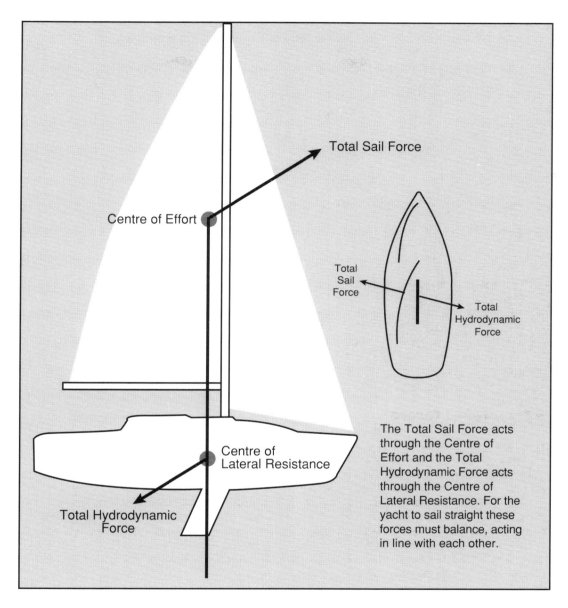

Total Sail Force

Centre of Effort

Total Sail Force

Total Hydrodynamic Force

Centre of Lateral Resistance

Total Hydrodynamic Force

The Total Sail Force acts through the Centre of Effort and the Total Hydrodynamic Force acts through the Centre of Lateral Resistance. For the yacht to sail straight these forces must balance, acting in line with each other.

the boat - be it in a straight line or round corners.

It is always better to set up the boat with a light amount of weather helm. Then, if you accidentally let go of the tiller, the boat will point into the wind and slow down. If you have lee helm it will bear away and pick up speed - perhaps even go into an accidental gybe. But light weather helm also increases the efficiency of the rudder in generating hydrodynamic force. That's because by turning the rudder to resist weather helm and keep the boat in a straight line, you are turning it so that it increases it's angle of attack to the water flow, compared to the keel. Because it is always acting in the turbulent flow from the keel, this increased angle of attack actually makes it more efficient in generating lift.

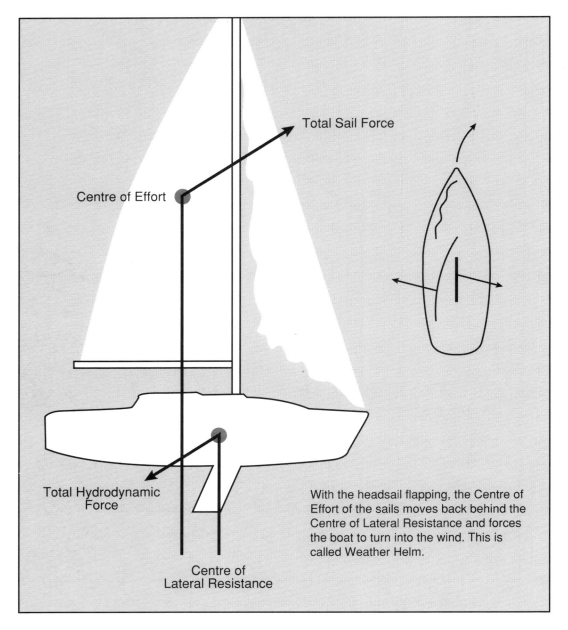

Total Sail Force

Centre of Effort

Total Hydrodynamic Force

Centre of Lateral Resistance

With the headsail flapping, the Centre of Effort of the sails moves back behind the Centre of Lateral Resistance and forces the boat to turn into the wind. This is called Weather Helm.

Conclusion

A short tour of the theory of sailing has shown us that sails are aerofoils, and that aerofoils can come in all shapes and sizes and be set at different angles of attack to the wind. Some of these angles and shapes are more efficient than others. We have also discovered that yachts sail by the balance of aerodynamic and hydrodynamic forces. So a book on sail trim should be all about changing the shape and angle of attack of our sails to balance these forces efficiently, to produce a light weather helm. And that's our starting point.

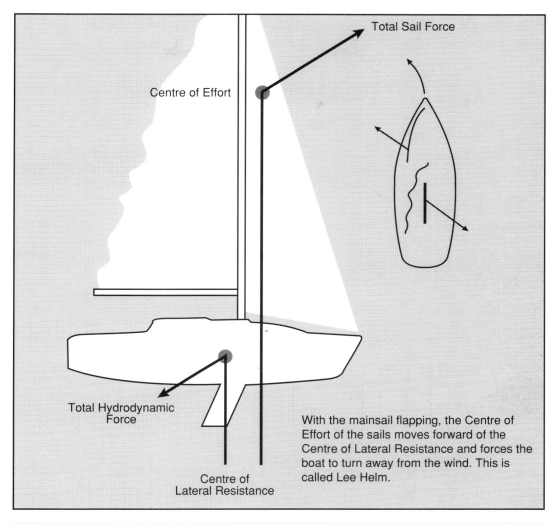

Total Sail Force

Centre of Effort

Total Hydrodynamic Force

Centre of Lateral Resistance

With the mainsail flapping, the Centre of Effort of the sails moves forward of the Centre of Lateral Resistance and forces the boat to turn away from the wind. This is called Lee Helm.

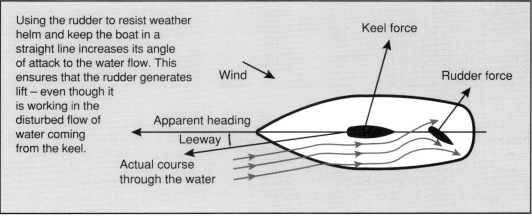

Using the rudder to resist weather helm and keep the boat in a straight line increases its angle of attack to the water flow. This ensures that the rudder generates lift – even though it is working in the disturbed flow of water coming from the keel.

Wind

Keel force

Rudder force

Apparent heading

Leeway

Actual course through the water

2 Seams and sailmakers

The principle

To understand how to set and trim (not to mention buy and maintain) your sails, we need an understanding of how they are put together. And this starts with the problem that every sailmaker faces.

Three-dimensional shapes from two-dimensional cloth

At the heart of sailmaking is the problem of creating a three-dimensional sail shape from flat, two-dimensional sailcloth. In principle there are two ways in which this could be done. One method is to mould a single piece of flexible material, and then set it in the required shape. This is only now becoming a practical possibility, and we will return to it briefly at the end of the chapter. The second method is to fasten a curved edge against a straight (or differently curved) one, keeping the same

overlap along the seam. When fastened like this, the two-dimensional flat panels force each other into a three-dimensional shape. You can test this for yourself with a couple of pieces of paper. This is how a sail is traditionally formed using the seams; carefully cut, separate flat panels are attached to each other in such a way that the required shape emerges.

The same principle is also used to force shape into the finished sail using the mast or the forestay. If the bend in the mast doesn't exactly match the curve in the luff of the sail, then shape is introduced in exactly the same way as shape is forced into the sail through the seams. Seam shaping and the luff curve/mast mismatch are analogous to a boatbuilder butting together panels with curved edges to create the hull shape from planks. But a moulded sail is analogous to the boatbuilder constructing in fibreglass.

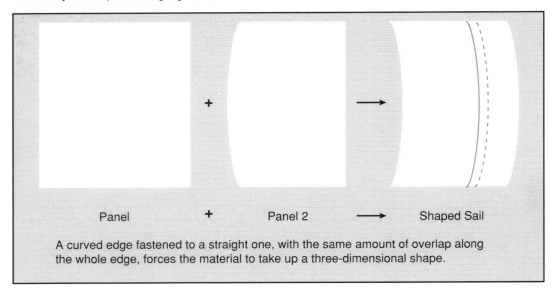

Panel   +   Panel 2   ⟶   Shaped Sail

A curved edge fastened to a straight one, with the same amount of overlap along the whole edge, forces the material to take up a three-dimensional shape.

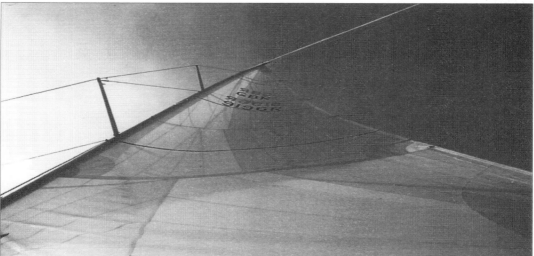

The same principle applies when an alteration in mast bend changes the shape of the sail.

The problem that the sailmaker faces that the boat builder doesn't is the need to change the shape. No sailboat carries a different sail for every additional knot of windspeed, yet if we were aiming for 100% performance even these small increments of change would require subtle alterations in the shape of the sail. The only way your sails can adapt to different conditions is by moving into different shapes. This is where stretch comes in. On the one hand too much stretch is bad, since it forces sails out of shape. On the other hand some stretch in your

sail is inevitable, and so the sailmaker must work with it to allow you to achieve the different sail shapes through sail trim.

The practice

So the sailmaker's job in building up the sail from panels is now complicated by two different requirements. Firstly, that the panels are cut and seamed to force the sail into the right shape; but secondly, that if the panels stretch under the loads from the wind and sail controls, they do so

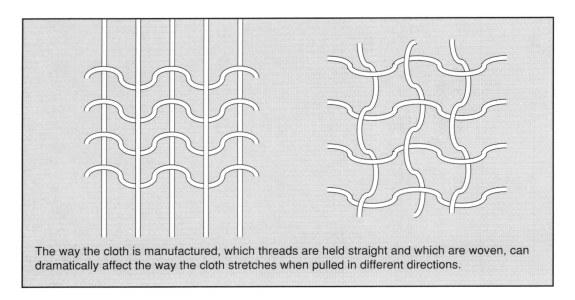

The way the cloth is manufactured, which threads are held straight and which are woven, can dramatically affect the way the cloth stretches when pulled in different directions.

in such a way that the different shapes forced into the sail are the right ones for the windspeed. This, as I'm sure you can imagine, is no easy task. Matters are simplified by the use of three basic panel layouts which are then varied to the needs of the particular boat. But before we can understand those, we need to look at the building blocks - the sailcloth.

Sailcloth

The vast majority of cruising sails are built with woven cloth, and any woven material has a fundamental property that is crucial to the sailmaker: it stretches differently depending on the direction you pull it in. You can demonstrate this to yourself by tugging at the cotton weave of a T-shirt or handkerchief; it stretches a great deal further if you pull it across the threads than along them. The explanation lies in the way the cloth is woven and that the threads, of necessity, pass under and over each other. Imagine that the threads in one direction are held completely straight, while those running at ninety degrees are woven and bent around them. If you pull the finished cloth along the line of the straight threads it will stretch very little. But if you pull it along the threads that are woven, those threads will be able to straighten a little, and so allow the cloth to stretch. If you pulled it at forty-five degrees to either threadline it would stretch

even more, since both thread directions can move against each other and there are no threads directly preventing stretch.

The cloth manufacturer can change the emphasis on which threads are held straightest when he weaves the cloth. Either threadline could be held completely straight, or both could 'weave' the same amount. This allows him to produce cloth with specific stretch properties that the sailmaker can then use in the sail design. These properties can be altered even further by changing the weight of the threads in the two directions. Making one of them much stronger than the other will obviously enhance the cloth's stretch resistance in that direction, compared to ninety degrees to it. But the direction which traditional woven sailcloth resists stretch the least is at forty-five degrees to both threadlines.

This led to two developments in sailcloth, the first of which was resin finishing the cloth. The idea is that the woven cloth is coated with a resin-type material that will hold the weave together and significantly enhance the thread's ability to resist moving against each other - the cause of the stretch off the threadline. This idea was taken one step further when the whole material was laminated in (glued between) a plastic film. These developments, along with a

Woven Polyester or Dacron is the standard material for cruising sails.

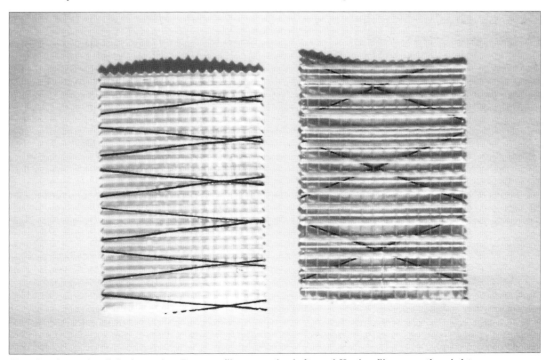

Two laminated sailcloths: using Dacron fibres on the left, and Kevlar fibres on the right.

whole range of new fibre materials, have dominated modern sailcloth.

Woven polyester

The main modern cruising sailcloth for upwind sails is woven polyester. This is often known as Dacron, Dacron being the polyester thread manufactured by DuPont. It can be finished in two ways; impregnated or coated with Melamine. Impregnating the fibres leads to a soft and manageable cloth that wears well, but doesn't have much resistance to stretch, particularly across the threadlines. The coat of Melamine adds to the stretch resistance as we've already described. But the downside with the finish is that it breaks down with use, and its ability to resist stretch breaks down with it. So resin- or Melamine-coated Dacron cloths have better stretch characteristics in the short term, but are less durable.

Laminates

The second main family of upwind sailcloths is the laminates, though these have had a very limited application in cruising sails, and few sailmakers would recommend them for this purpose. Various synthetic fibres are laminated between two Mylar films in a manufacturing process that can involve high pressure and heat. As with the Melamine finish, the Mylar laminate reduces the amount of stretch due to the nature of woven material. The film helps stop the interlocking fibres moving and straightening under load. But the Mylar film is even more vulnerable to being cracked when the sail is flogged or trodden on, and once it is cracked it is not supplying the same strength to the weave. So while it provides a very stable, strong and light cloth, its durability is very limited compared to woven Dacron. This is why it is used in racing sails, where performance is more important than durability.

Fibres

A similar story can be told about the fibres. Dacron remains the fibre of choice for cruising sails because of its low cost and high resistance to wear - by handling, salt water and sunlight.

A cross-cut mainsail.

Other fibres provide greater strength or less stretch, but are far less durable. We can include all the aramid fibres in this category, which you will see as the brand names Kevlar, Twaron and Technora. Even more exotic are Vectran and Zylon or PBO, and they are also more expensive and fragile, but provide racing sailors with the resistance to stretch that they need.

The exception to all these costly exotic materials is Spectra or Dyneema - which is the same fibre from different manufacturers. Their resistance to both sunlight and breakdown from handling makes them a good option for cruising sails. Their only limitation is Spectra's tendency to 'creep' under high loads and with time - that is deform and not return to the original shape. This means that your sails may slowly and irretrievably lose their shape, but they will be highly durable. Again the cruising sailor's interest in durability rather than performance separates them from the keen racer.

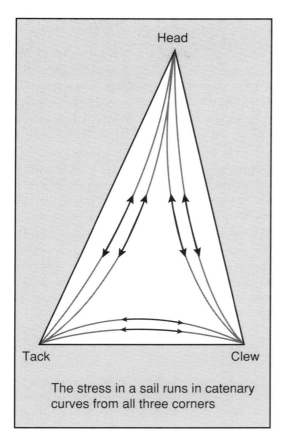

Head

Tack

Clew

The stress in a sail runs in catenary
curves from all three corners

Spinnaker cloth

Spinnaker cloth is a woven, finished material just
like the woven Dacron in upwind sails. In fact it
is possible to make spinnakers out of a polyester
cloth. Polyester is stronger and more stable than
the Nylon alternative, resisting stretch and
remaining dimensionally stable under changes
in temperature and humidity. But because of this
lack of 'give' it is not so good at the kind of shock
loading involved in spinnaker flying - such as
sudden filling after collapsing or during a set.
For this reason cruising spinnakers are normally
built from a nylon cloth of the appropriate
weight for the boat. Nylon is a much more
forgiving spinnaker cloth. It has a high tear
strength combined with a soft finish, and its
ability to withstand shock loads also makes it
forgiving when set and trimmed.

Construction

So much for the sailcloth, how do we put it
together to make a sail?

Cross cut

Until the early eighties all modern sails were
built using a cross-cut panel layout, where the
shaping is introduced into the sail using
horizontal panels and seams. The disadvantage
with this is that the main loads in the sail run
vertically, spreading out from each of the
corners. Computer techniques developed in
the last fifteen years allow us to calculate these
loads and their distribution through the sail.
Using this we can see that the load will run
through the cross-cut panels at different angles,
and we have already seen how (particularly)
woven cloth will stretch differently when pulled
at different angles to the threads. This difference
in stretch through the panels can lead to
distortion unless the sail is reinforced or made
from heavier material. This problem led the
racing sailors to look for a solution, and they
came up with two other panel layouts that are
just as applicable to the cruising sailor.

Bi-radial and tri-radial

The fundamental idea behind both bi-radial and
tri-radial panel layouts is that the panels are
placed, as far as possible, in line with the loads
in the sail. Since these loads run radially out of
the sail's corners, so do the panels, which is
where the name comes from. Bi-radial sails have
radial panels running from the head and the
clew, which are the two most heavily loaded
corners. The tri-radial design uses radial panels
in the tack as well. This is more important in
headsails where the tack loading is relatively
higher than in a mainsail. The radial design
means that each panel can be matched precisely
to the load, so that the stretch is carefully
controlled. The result is a much smoother sail,
less prone to distortion, which can be built more
lightly for the same strength.

Variations on a theme

Almost all cruising sails are built to cross-cut,

A bi-radial panel layout in a headsail, with panels radiating from the head and the clew.

A tri-radial panel layout in a headsail, with panels radiating from the head, the clew and the tack.

bi-radial and tri-radial sail designs. But there are a couple of alternative methods, proprietary sail manufacturing systems, that you may see advertised or on the masts of our racing brethren. These variations on the main theme use laminated sailcloth. The sails are built with the fibres directly orientated to the loads, within a cross-cut system of Mylar panels. At the moment few, if any, sailmakers would recommend laminated material for cruising

sails, even in these new forms. It simply isn't durable enough. And so we will touch on these sails, some of which are built on the principle of the moulded sail we mentioned at the beginning, only to pass them by.

Spinnakers

As with spinnaker cloth, the panel layouts and constructions are extensions of the ideas we have already discussed. The simplest option would be to build the sail to a cross-cut design, with horizontal seaming. But the radial design has the same advantages for spinnakers as it does for upwind sails, allowing the sail designer more freedom to accommodate the complex curves of a spinnaker shape and match the stresses to the thread lines. A radial head and cross-cut bottom is a very practical option. More refined is the full tri-radial sail, with all three corners having radial panels which meet at a centre seam.

Fully battened or soft battened?

Adding battens to a sail is a reinforcement for the cloth. Intelligently placed and carefully engineered battens will help the sail hold its shape and resist the flogging that breaks down the cloth. The question of how many battens and how long they should be (full length or not) crosses over into the sail handling discussion we will be having later. If you choose in-mast furling you can't have any battens at all, never mind full-length ones. Suffice to say here that the use of battens greatly increases the sail's ability to hold its shape both over time and with increasing wind strength. The improvement in durability and performance is offset by increases in cost and weight of the sail.

3 Sail shape as a science

Sail shape, like sail construction, has become a much more scientific affair in recent years. The development of a simple photographic technique to measure sail shape, and the subsequent computerisation of that process, has allowed sailors and sailmakers to move on from reliance on the human eye. Eyeballing sail shape has only ever been a consistent way of trimming sails if you spend a lot of time doing it. For the rest of us there are more 'hands on' techniques, and they will form the basis of the remaining chapters in this book. But there are some useful general lessons to be learned from a brief review of sail shape analysis.

Seeing sail shape

When you are sailing upwind with the sails trimmed to their normal position, stand about half-way along the boom and look up at the shape along a line parallel to the boom, about half-way up the mainsail. Sail numbers or a horizontal seam may help you see the shape.

Often racing boats have coloured stripes along the sail to make the shape more visible. You can see the headsail shape by lying on your back on the foredeck to get the right view. But you may well need oilskins for this operation unless there is light air and flat water! What you are trying to assess is how deep the sail is at the point of maximum depth, and where that depth is in relation to the width of the sail. You will have to imagine a straight line running from the leech to the luff of the sail, and compare the distance of the sail from that line all the way along it. It's more scientific if you have a camera with you, and you can take photographs looking up the sail. The disposable waterproof cameras that are now available are perfect for this task.

Seeing twist

In looking at the shape of the sails, we can also assess the degree of twist. We can see that for the foot of the mainsail the boom is the same as the imaginary line from the luff to the leech from

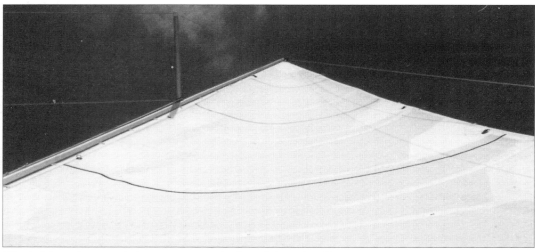

The twist can be seen to increase as you look up this mainsail.

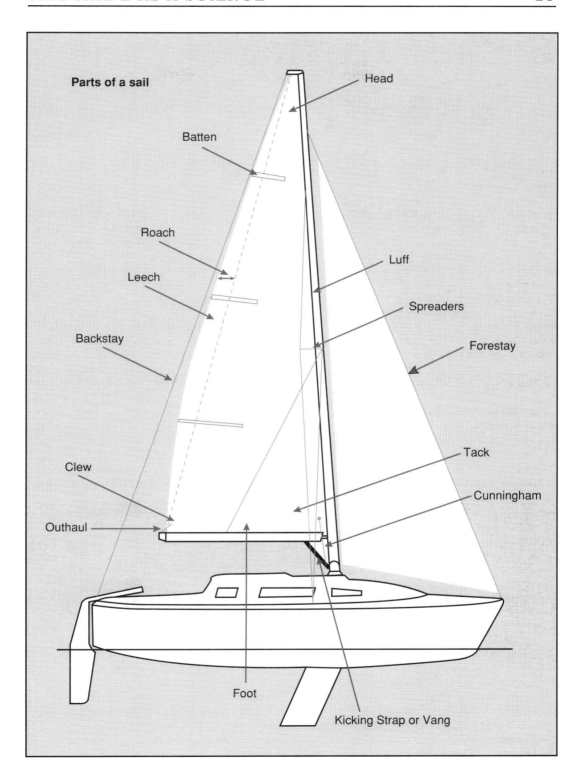

Parts of a sail

Head

Batten

Roach

Leech

Backstay

Luff

Spreaders

Forestay

Clew

Tack

Cunningham

Outhaul

Foot

Kicking Strap or Vang

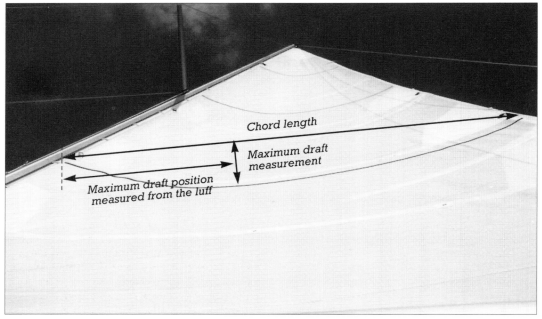

We can measure the position of maximum draft and the depth from the photograph, as follows:

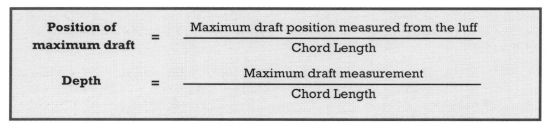

Position of maximum draft	=	Maximum draft position measured from the luff
		Chord Length
Depth	=	Maximum draft measurement
		Chord Length

which we assess the sail depth. Try sailing upwind with the boom on or close to the centreline of the boat - pointing from bow to stern. Looking up the mainsail, the imaginary line from luff to leech points further off to leeward as you go up the sail. The amount that it points to leeward is called the degree of twist. You should be able to see this increasing twist all the way up the sail.

Defining and measuring shape

Sailmakers talk about the deepest point of the sail as the maximum draft, and where that point is located on the sail as the position of maximum draft. The sail width is called the chord, which is the name for the width of any aero- or hydro-foil. We can measure all of these things from a

photograph of the sail and can then calculate a couple of percentages that are fundamental to the science of sail shape.

Some sail shape guidelines

Every sail can have its shape described by two numbers (defined above) for three different heights on the sail; at one third, half and two thirds of the way up the sail. The maximum variation in draft position and depth for the majority of sailing yachts, across all upwind sails and in all conditions, is only about 12%. Maximum draft position ranges from 38% to 50%, and the depth from 8% to 20%. It takes a great deal of practice to see these small variations in shape. Fortunately, as we have already seen, there are other ways of tackling the problem. Nevertheless, it would be well worth doing a photographic analysis of your own sails to see if they fall within these parameters when they are trimmed to their normal settings.

Unfortunately, it is impossible to be much more precise about the shape you want for any given sail on your boat: there are too many other variables to take into account - the design, displacement and rig for instance. In twelve to fifteen knots they should fall somewhere in the band of figures that we've given. If they don't, then hopefully the advice on trim in the rest of the book will allow you to improve the shape. But there are limits to the amount the sail shape can be altered through sail trim. And if, after your subsequent efforts, they still don't match the figures, then the sails may well be worn out and due for replacement. If they are less than a season old, you might want to change your sailmaker!

General rules for sail shape

We can also make some general rules about how the sail shape should vary, both through the sail and through the wind range. None of these rules tackles how much, when or where sail trim should vary with the conditions. That will come from our set of practical trimming techniques. But using the photographic method to check your normal sail trim against these rules would be an excellent way to start your sail trimming career. Alternatively, assessing the differences in shape by eye, and how they compare to these rules, will also help you to build up a memory for sail shapes.

1. On both the mainsail and the headsail the sail should be flatter at the bottom than at the top.

2. On both the mainsail and the headsail the depth should be further forward at the bottom than the top.

3. As the wind increases the depth should move forward, and the sail should get flatter.

4. As the wind decreases, the depth should move back, and the sail should get fuller, until very light air (1 or 2 knots), when it should be flat again.

5. At any wind speed, looking at the same height (one third, half or two thirds height) the depth should be fuller and further forward in headsails than in mainsails.

Changing shapes

We are almost ready to get down to the practical elements of sail trim, but there is one more fundamental we need to look at. And that's the principles behind altering the shape of a sail. We have already seen that the sail is designed so that any stretch in the cloth allows us to control the sail shape. This works by pulling on the corners and down and along the edges of the sails to put tension into the cloth in those areas. The sail responds to this tension in one of two ways: either the maximum draft position moves towards the edge you are pulling along, and/or the sail flattens along that edge.

We also know that some of the shape in the sail is forced into it by the difference between the curve of the luff of the sail and the curve of the mast or headstay. So it follows that changing the mastbend or headstay tension will alter the shape of the sail. This is the case, and the design should ensure that the cloth stretch will accommodate this sail shape alteration.

Using the information in this chapter, you could work out sail trim from first principles - and a lot of trial and error! You'll be relieved to hear that there is an easier way, and that's what we'll now move on to. But keep all this in mind, because it's the basis of everything that we will now look at.

This headsail is set-up for medium conditions with the position of maximum depth further forward at the bottom than the top. Taken at the same time as the mainsail, we can also see the position of maximum depth is further forward, and the headsail is fuller than the mainsail at each comparable sail stripe.

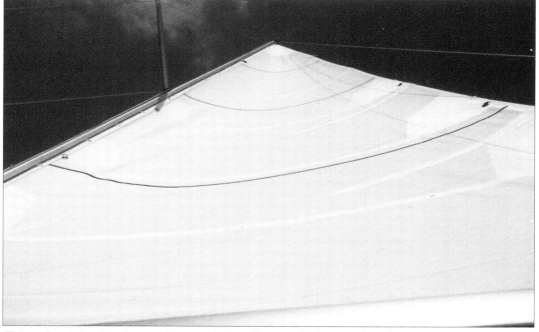

This mainsail is set up for medium conditions, flatter at the bottom than the top.

In lighter air the headsail is set-up with the position of maximum depth further aft than for medium conditions, and the sail is fuller.

4 Controlling sail shape

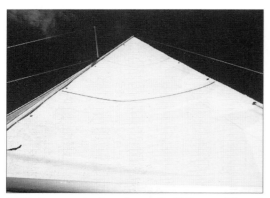 

With the cunningham loose (left) the position of maximum draft is further aft than when the cunningham is pulled on tight (right).

Sail trim controls allow us to alter the shape of the sails, and their angle of attack to the wind. In this chapter we are going to look at how they work and what they do.

The mainsail

The controls used on the mainsail are the same as those for any other sail set from a mast - such as a mizzen.

The halyard and cunningham

The mainsail halyard isn't there just to pull the sail up: it also allows us to tension the luff of the sail. Because there is a limit to how hard you can pull on the mainsail halyard before the sail is at the top of its hoist, racing boats often fit a cunningham. This is a block and tackle or rope/winch system that allows tension to be applied down the luff of the sail at the tack. It has exactly the same effect as the halyard but is easier to pull on and let off, and much greater control can be had over the sail shape, because much greater tension can be applied. When you increase the tension with the halyard or cunningham you will pull the depth forward in the sail. This will also make the sail flatter at the leech, and slightly flatten the sail overall.

The outhaul

The outhaul applies tension along the foot in exactly the same way as the cunningham or halyard does to the luff, but the effect is different. Modern sail design has made it impossible for the outhaul to pull the draft in the sail towards the foot, and the affect of the outhaul is to flatten the mainsail in the lower third.

The vang (kicking strap)

Both the foot and the luff are connected to spars - the boom and the mast. The leech is different, because it's unsupported. The most important consequence of this is that more than one control affects tension in the leech - it's a combination of the mainsheet and the vang. The vang is pulling down on the boom and hence tensioning the leech directly, whereas the primary role for the mainsheet

With the outhaul loose (bottom) the mainsail is much fuller in the bottom third than when the outhaul is tight (top).

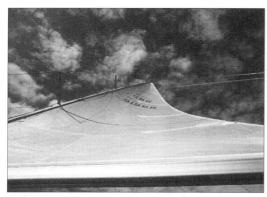 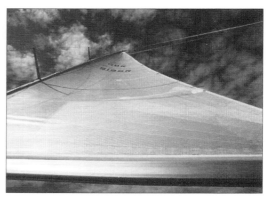

With the vang loose (left) the mainsail has considerably more twist than when it is tight (right).

A common style of traveller and mainsheet system aboard a cruising boat.

is setting the angle of attack of the mainsail. Whichever device is used, putting tension on the leech initially affects the twist in the sail. Once the twist is reduced to the minimum possible for the wind conditions, the sailcloth will start to stretch down the leech, and this tension will pull the draft in the sail backwards.

But a significant amount of force will have to be exerted to achieve this, and the vang, because it is attached to the boom so near the mast, may not be capable of it.

The mainsheet

The main job of the mainsheet is to set the angle of attack of the mainsail. It is helped in this by the traveller, which of course complicates matters further, since the mainsheet is already helping the vang with the leech tension. It's a simplification of all the possibilities, but we can say that when the mainsail is eased off the centreline of the boat, the mainsheet is primarily responsible for controlling the angle of attack of the mainsail. During this period the vang is controlling the leech tension and therefore the twist in the sail. Once the boom is pulled into the middle of the boat, the mainsheet's effect is transferred to tightening the leech and controlling the twist. And because the mainsheet is so much more powerful a system than the vang, it will be capable of taking over from the vang and tensioning the leech to the point where the draft will move aft. The traveller is now primarily responsible for the angle of attack of the mainsail.

The traveller

The traveller is a thwarthships-mounted track, with a 'travelling' car on which the lower purchase of the mainsheet system is usually mounted. By dragging the mainsheet up and down the track, it can be used to alter the angle of attack of the mainsail to the wind. But it is most useful upwind, as we have seen, when the mainsheet is tight and controlling the leech tension. The traveller can then be used to alter the angle of attack of the sail, without also affecting the leech tension.

The headsail

In comparison to the mainsail, the headsail is only directly attached along one edge, rather than two, which makes controlling the shape more difficult. The same set of sail controls apply to any other sail set from a single flexible stay, such as a staysail.

The halyard

Tension is put on the luff by the headsail halyard, in exactly the same way as the main halyard or cunningham works on the mainsail. So tightening the headsail halyard pulls the draft forward, and easing it allows the draft to return back aft.

> Trimmers talk about 'on' and 'off'.
> 'On' means tighter; 'trim on' means wind in the control line under discussion.
> 'Off' means ease out the control line.

The headsail sheet

As with the mainsail sheet, pulling on the headsail sheet when the headsail is eased is primarily affecting the angle of attack to the wind. But as the sheet gets tighter, it starts to affect both the tension on the foot and the leech. How much tension is directed up which edge will depend on where the sheet is positioned on the deck - which is known as the lead position. Tensioning the leech will affect the twist in the sail exactly as it does on the mainsail, until the cloth starts to stretch when the draft will be pulled aft. Tensioning the foot will flatten the sail out in the lower

A fore-and-aft track for controlling the headsail lead position.

third, just as the outhaul does for the mainsail. It is impossible to separate the work of the headsail sheet from that of the lead position. The two must be juggled together to provide the right balance of leech and foot tension, and angle of attack

The lead position

The point where the headsail sheet hits the deck is known as the lead position. This is critical to the trim of the sail. The lead position is usually altered fore-and-aft by a moveable car on a track. Ideally you would have more than one track, or a barber-hauler system that also allowed you to move the lead position inboard and outboard. A barber-hauler is just a rope attached directly to the sheet, then led to a winch and tensioned to pull the sheet, and hence the lead position, inboard or outboard. Some boats may have tracks

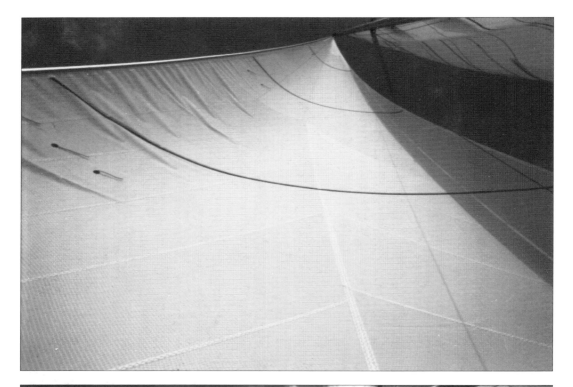

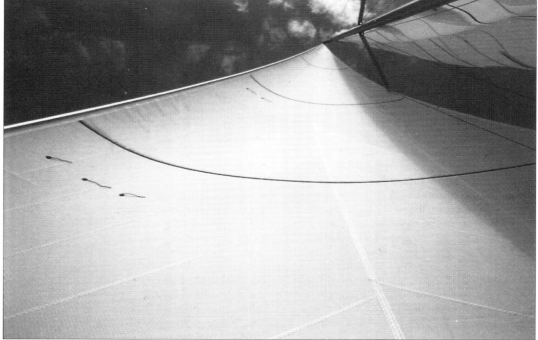

With the headsail halyard loose (top) the draft is further aft in the sail than with it tight (below).

A lateral track for controlling the headsail lead position. This is combined with height adjustment, to give effective control over the fore and aft position as well.

that move laterally rather than fore-and-aft, and perhaps incorporate this with a system for letting the lead up and down. Letting the lead position move up and down has the same effect as moving it fore-and-aft.

The lead position determines whether the sheet tension is applied most strongly to the foot or the leech. The further back in the boat the lead is, the harder the sheet will pull on the foot. Conversely, the further forward the lead is, the harder the sheet will pull on the leech. Moving the lead position across the boat laterally can also affect the angle of attack of the headsail.

As with the mainsail we can try and simplify the changing roles of the two controls. When the jib is eased on a reach the sheet is controlling the angle of attack of the sail, with some help from the lead position if it can

be moved outboard. While the sheet directly controls the tension in the leech and the foot, it is the lead position that affects the relative tension applied to each. This `balance of power' continues until the headsail is sheeted on hard for sailing upwind. Now the sheet still controls the tension in foot and leech. And the lead position still controls the relative tension in each through its fore-and-aft position. But the lead position has taken over responsibility for the angle of attack of the sail, through its lateral position. The sheet cannot be used to do this, since it cannot be eased sufficiently to have any effect.

Mast bend and headstay tension

For a racing sailor mast bend and headstay tension are fundamental to the shape of the main and headsail. For a cruising sailor they

More mast bend than luff curve in the mainsail means a flat sail (left), and less mast bend than luff curve means a fuller sail (right).

are much less important. This means that you have substantially less control over sail shape than the racing sailor - but it also means you are much less likely to lose the mast!

Mast bend

Most genuine cruising boats, as opposed to the cross-bred cruiser/racers, have masts that are designed to bend very little, if at all. So we will not be dealing with mast bend in any detail. If you have a bendy cruiser/racer rig, and want to know more about setting it up, then you need a racing book such as Tuning Yachts & Small Keelboats by Lawrie Smith (also published by Fernhurst Books). We would define a bendy rig as one with more than four or five inches of bend over the length of a forty foot luff. You can measure mast bend precisely by pulling the main halyard tight between the sheave and the

gooseneck, and then sending someone aloft to measure the gap between the halyard and the back of the track. This distance is the mast bend.

The effect of mast bend on the mainsail is directly related to the amount of luff curve in the sail. If you lay a new mainsail out flat on the floor you will see that the luff rope lies in a convex curve; this is the luff curve. The mast bend should match the luff curve of the sail. When the mainsail is hoisted, if the luff curve matches the mast bend the sail will set on the rig without the mast inducing any shape in the sail. But if there is more bend in the mast than there is in the sail, the mast will force the sail to take up a flatter shape than it otherwise would. Conversely, if there is less bend in the mast than the luff curve, the mast will force the sail to take up a fuller shape.

It follows from this that if we bend or straighten the mast while we are sailing we can alter the fullness or power of the mainsail - and this is exactly what racing sailors are so preoccupied with. But for the limited bend of a cruising mast, your only real concern is whether the sail and the mast are mismatched.

Over bend

If the mast is bending too much for the luff curve of the mainsail then the sail will suffer from what is called luff starvation. The symptom of luff starvation is the creases that run out of the clew of the mainsail towards the middle of the mast. The cure is either to get the mainsail re-cut with more luff curve, or to straighten the mast. If the creases only appear occasionally when you are sailing, there may be a simple cure. If you have a masthead rig with a topmast backstay (or a fractional rig with running backstays) then try easing them; this will reduce the mast bend and

may cure the problem. If it doesn't then you will need to change something more fundamental in the mast set-up. Try moving the mast foot forward on the keel, or back at the deck level, or altering spreaders or rig tension. Most cruising boats are not set up for this kind of alteration, and it may well require some major engineering. In this instance it is a lot easier to get your sailmaker to come out and have a look, or even take him some photos of the sail, and have the luff curve re-cut. It's a quick job, and the racing guys do it all the time, often overnight.

Too straight

If the mast is too straight the sail will be too full at the front. In a really bad case this might be obvious, but it's much more likely that the symptoms are more subtle and will only emerge through handling and trimming problems - which we will meet in the next chapters.

Increasing the bend in a mast is done by reversing the process above - put more tension on the backstay, or adjust the mast foot, deck chocking or rigging. Once again if you feel you have a real problem, then re-cutting the sail is almost certainly simpler than everything except changing the backstay tension.

Headstay tension

As with mast bend, headstay tension is a different deal on a racing boat, this time because of their powerful backstay systems. The use of headstay foils also makes the head-stay and sail work better as a unit and the result is precise control of both the headstay tension and sail shape. But few cruising boats have either a racing-style headstay foil or the facility to get the headstay particularly tight. This means that the headstay will always be sagging to leeward, more so in stronger winds and if the sail is hanked on. The headsail should be designed to allow for this. If you lay the headsail out flat on the ground you will see that, as with the mainsail, the luff is curved. It should be concave, not convex, to match the headstay sag.

If the luff curve doesn't match the headstay sag then the headstay will force shape into the sail. Straightening the headstay more than the luff curve will make the headsail flatter. Letting the headstay sag more than the luff curve will make the sail fuller. Symptoms of either case will only appear through the process of trimming the sail, and so they will be dealt with in the next chapter, which is all about trimming headsails.

5 Headsail trimming

This chapter is about headsail trimming upwind and off the wind as far as beam reaching. Trimming downwind is covered in Chapter 9. We will assume moderate conditions, 8 to 12 knots of true wind speed (the speed of the wind blowing past you if you were just drifting on the water) for our first time out. Sail trimming can be considered a process with a beginning and an end, and that process starts with setting up the headsail. The gadget that allows us to turn theory into practical headsail trim is the telltale.

Telltales

Telltales are the biggest aid to sail trim. A telltale is a light piece of material, attached to both sides of the sail, or threaded through it and knotted in place. On the headsail there should be three sets, about a foot back from the luff, one set at each of one third, half and two thirds the height of the sail. Typically they are made from wool, ribbon or audio tape.

Once the telltales are on the sail and the sail is up and sheeted on, you will see that they are either flying, or drooping (sometimes called lifting). If the telltale is flying that means the air is flowing over that side of the sail as it should. If the telltale is drooping or lifting that means there is no steady air flow over that side of the sail. The sail is stalled. The objective behind headsail trimming is to get all three sets of telltales on the headsail flying on both sides of the sail. To help us achieve that, we have three rules for using telltales on a headsail.

Three rules for using headsail telltales

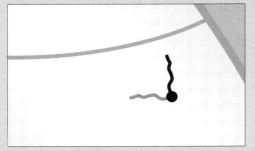 

(left) The windward telltales are drooping or lifting and the leeward telltales flying - pull the sail in or bear away. (right) The leeward telltales lifting and the windward telltales flying - ease out the sail or luff up.

Rule 1 - Steering to telltales

To adjust your steering to get both windward and leeward telltales flying, look at just the bottom set:

If the windward one droops, bear away or steer away from the wind to get it to fly.

If the leeward one droops, luff up or steer closer to the wind to get it to fly.

Three rules for using headsail telltales (cont.)

Rule 2 - Trimming to telltales

To adjust the sail to get both windward and leeward telltales flying, look at just the bottom set:

If the windward telltale is flying but not the leeward one - ease the sheet.

If the leeward telltale is flying but not the windward one - pull in the sheet.

Rule 3 - Telltales working vertically

To get all three sets of telltales to work together vertically (so that if the bottom windward telltale is drooping the middle and top windward telltales will be as well), you need to adjust the lead position. Look at all three sets:

If the windward telltale is flying at the top, but the bottom one is drooping, move the sheet lead position aft.

If the windward telltale is flying at the bottom, but not the top, move the sheet lead position forward.

With these three rules in mind, we can now look at setting up the headsail to sail both upwind and off-the-wind.

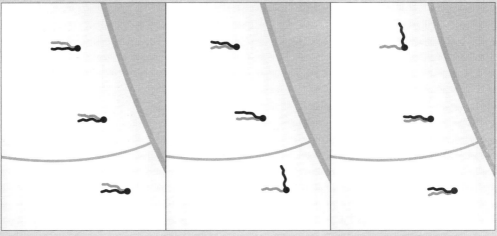

All three sets of telltales working together vertically, and starting to lift at exactly the same moment.

The windward tell-tale is flying at the top, but the bottom one is lifting, so move the sheet lead position aft.

The windward telltale is flying at the bottom, but not the top, so move the sheet lead forward.

Sailing upwind

Turn the boat onto an upwind course, and pull the headsail in (or 'sheet on' as the jargon has it) until the foot of the sail is just touching the shroud. As you do so, check that the sail is not tight against the rig anywhere further up - you don't want to poke a spreader through the sail! Firstly check out the sail shape by eye: is the maximum draft at least fifty percent forward? If not, wind on some more halyard to move it forward. If it is much fuller than those shown in our pictures, then if you have a masthead rig put the topmast backstay on tight - this will hold the headstay up to windward and flatten the sail. (The running backstay does the same job on a fractional rig.) You may need to ask the boat-builder or mast maker how tight you can pull on the backstay; by fifteen knots of true wind speed it should be as tight as the structure will allow.

Sail upwind with the helmsman watching the bottom set of telltales and steering according to Rule 1. The trimmer should be watching all three sets of telltales and trying to see if he needs to adjust the lead position according to Rule 3. Sometimes it helps if the helmsman luffs gently to windward. All three sets of telltales should lift together. If they don't, use Rule 3 to adjust the lead position. Once you have the lead position correct the helmsman can steer upwind using Rule 1, and you can be confident that your headsail trim is accurate.

But sometimes you will find that wherever you put the lead, the telltales refuse to work together vertically. This is because the sail is fundamentally the wrong shape. It is too full in either the bottom or the top compared to the rest of the sail, either because it was built that way, or it stretched irreparably into that shape through use. However much you pull it about, you will not be able to fix it with the trim. At this point you can either shrug your shoulders and put the kettle on knowing you've done your best, get a sailmaker to re-cut the headsail, or buy a new one.

Sailing off the wind

When you are sailing off the wind you are almost invariably sailing to a course, which is most likely the compass heading to where you want to go. We will use this as the starting point.

Once the boat is settled on a course, sheet the headsail on using Rule 2. You may find that you have a lot of heel, or that the headsail is a very round shape (another symptom is the mainsail backwinding, but we will come to this in the next chapter). This will most likely be the case if you are beam reaching or close to it. What you need to do to improve the sail shape and flatten the boat is move the lead outboard towards the side of the boat. The rule of thumb is that upwind the headsail lead position is on the normal track, and by the time you are beam reaching the lead position should be as far outboard as it can go. This is where the barber hauler or lateral tracks are so useful, allowing you to pull the lead outboard quickly and easily.

With the lateral lead position settled, you can trim the sheet according to Rule 2, and then start checking that the three telltales are working together vertically. If you need help to see which one is lifting first, get the helmsman to luff gently above the course. Then use Rule 3 to set the fore-and-aft lead position. You are now set and trimmed efficiently to get to your destination - at least until the wind direction or speed changes, when you will need to re-adjust things. If the wind comes more on the beam then ease the sheet, if it blows from closer to the bow sheet on. But in every case the telltales will tell you what to do provided you follow our three trimming rules.

With the headsail lead too far inboard for a reach the bottom of the sail is very round and the wind is flowing straight off it into the mainsail. As a consequence the mainsail is over-sheeted.

With the headsail lead further outboard the bottom of the sail is more open. We have been able to ease the main a little and the leeches of both sails are close to being parallel all the way down.

This headsail is too full.

Here it has more headstay tension, which flattens the sail and gets it closer to the shrouds.

6 Mainsail trimming

Although this mainsail has a tell-tale at every batten, you only really need one at the top.

Mainsail and headsail trimmed nicely for reaching in a medium breeze.

In this chapter we'll look at mainsail trimming upwind, and off the wind as far as a beam reach. It is the final part of the process that we started in Chapter 5.

Mainsail telltales

First a comment on mainsail telltales. They don't work on the main in the same way as they work on the headsail because of the interaction of the two sails and the mast. You only really need one telltale on the mainsail, and that is stitched onto the leech at the top batten. Once that's in place, you're ready to go.

Off the wind

Sailing off the wind we'll assume, as we will throughout this chapter, that the headsail is already trimmed according to Chapter 5, and the boat is being steered on course. Ease the halyard or the cunningham so that the luff is completely slack. The outhaul can be eased, but not so far that wrinkles appear along the foot of the sail. Then drop the traveller or ease the mainsheet until you just start to see backwind along the luff of the sail - backwind is air redirected off the headsail that is blowing the luff of the main to windward. The backwind may appear before the main is eased enough to keep the boat at the right angle of heel. If the leeward sidedeck is in the water it's forcing the boat to heel too much. This is because the headsail is creating too much backwind - the lead position needs to be moved further outboard as we mentioned in Chapter 5. You should then be able to ease the mainsheet more and get the boat to a comfortable angle of heel.

Now pull on the vang until the last ten inches of the top batten is nearly parallel to the boom. This means you have just the right amount of twist. You can assess this most easily by looking up from under the boom to see if the two are in line. If pulling the vang on this far puts the end of the boom close to the water, ease the vang back off a little. If it remains a problem, you are heeling too much and you have too much sail up. Similarly, if both the sails are eased out as far as the telltales and backwinding will let them, you shouldn't have a problem with rudder balance when you are reaching. If you do it's because either the headsail is too big (lee helm) or the mainsail is too big (weather helm). We will look at reducing sail in Chapter 7.

Sailing upwind

Trimming the mainsail upwind is all about responding to the headsail trim to balance the boat. Rudder balance, and the concept of weather or lee helm that we discussed in Chapter 1, is fundamental to upwind mainsail trim.

To start the process pull on the outhaul as tight as you can. Then have a look at the sail shape - where is the maximum draft position? Pull on the cunningham or tighten the halyard if you need to move the draft forward. Then set the traveller slightly to windward of the centreline. Pull on the mainsheet until the end of the top batten is parallel to the boom (again look up from under the boom to check). The boom should now be close to or on the centreline of the boat. If it isn't pull the traveller up until the end of the boom is on the centreline. Look up at the top batten leech telltale: it should now be flying 80% of the time (so occasionally you should see it flick behind the mainsail). There should be no

Mainsail and headsail trimmed nicely for beating upwind in medium conditions.

backwind from the headsail and a light tug of weather helm on the wheel or tiller. If this is the case, you are at or very close to your optimum upwind trim - congratulations!

Unfortunately the chances of it all going this smoothly are slim, and even if you have achieved the correct trim, more or less wind will change things. We'll now look at the responses to the most likely problems. As far as is possible, they are in order of importance. But as you will see, everything is interactive - changing one thing affects all the others.

Ocean Leopard has everything trimmed nicely, but there's just too much sail up and the boat is heeled too far, with the leeward rail in the water. But it looks like they're just about to change to a smaller sail.

Too much heel

If the leeward sidedeck is buried in the water, but everything else in your trim is correct, then you have too much sail up - turn to Chapter 7. But if there's too much heel and something else is also wrong, then fix the other problem first. If, after you have sorted out all the other problems below, you still have too much heel, again you should shorten sail according to Chapter 7.

Too much weather helm

Too much weather helm means one hand on the wheel or tiller isn't enough to keep the boat going in a straight line. If you are fighting the weather helm, drop the traveller to leeward until it goes away. If the traveller goes all the way to leeward and you still have too much weather helm, ease the mainsheet. You may find that this corrects the weather helm, but that now the

With the traveller too far to windward the yacht has a lot of weather helm as you can see from the rudder angle and the wash (left). Dropping the traveller to leeward gets rid of the weather helm, the rudder straightens and the wash flattens out (right). This is quicker and more comfortable.

Here the mainsail is backwinding too much.

Flattening the mainsail and retrimming the headsail, in particular moving the lead aft, sorts out the problem.

mainsail is backwinding, in which case see below. Possibly the mainsail will not be backwinding (or you cure the backwinding as below), but the leech telltale is always flying, and the top batten is no longer parallel to the boom. Instead the top batten is too open - the outboard end is pointing to leeward.

In this case the mainsail is too powerful, not so much that you really need to reef, but enough that flattening the mainsail would help. You can pull on both more outhaul and more cunningham, which will flatten the sail. It will allow you to pull the sheet harder and still keep the helm balanced. If you have a reasonably powerful topmast backstay on a masthead rig, then you can put more backstay on: this may bend the mast a little and flatten the sail (the

running backstays will do the same for a fractional rig).

Too much mainsail backwinding

It is possible to live with a little mainsail backwinding; it's no problem if the luff lifts every thirty seconds or so when you get a gust of wind. But often you will find that before the helm and heel are correct, there is a lot of backwind on the mainsail from the headsail. The mainsail may be flogging intermittently. When that happens the helm will become very unbalanced, and you may find that you have lee helm on occasions! First check that the mainsail is as depowered as you can get it, as we did above (pull on the cunningham, outhaul and backstay). Then we must adjust the headsail trim

With the traveller too far to leeward the yacht has lee helm - you can see the tiller is pushed to leeward trying to keep the yacht on the wind. You definitely want to get rid of this by pulling the traveller to windward.

to settle the mainsail. First ease the headsail sheet a couple of inches. If that doesn't fix it, move the lead aft a few inches. If it's still a problem move the lead outboard six inches. Don't worry about the effect this has on the headsail telltales. If you still have a backwind problem after these changes, you need a smaller headsail. So either furl some up or change to a smaller sail: again, Chapter 7 deals with this in more detail.

Lee helm

This is something you definitely want to get rid of, so pull the traveller to windward to correct it. If you end up with the boom on the centreline

and still have lee helm, then sheet on the mainsail. It's possible that you will have to oversheet the mainsail to get weather helm, and you will see this because the leech telltale is always stalling and the top batten is closed (ie the outboard end is pointing to windward rather than parallel to the boom). These all tell you that the headsail is too powerful compared to the main. If you have flattened the mainsail off by pulling on the cunningham and outhaul, or by tensioning the backstay, ease them back to where they were. If you have a reef in the mainsail, shake it out.

If you still have lee helm when you have done that, you must try and depower the headsail.

Move the headsail lead position aft, and then
outboard (but no more than 6-8 inches on either
of them). If you still have lee helm after you have
done all that, you need a smaller headsail.

The trimming process is a loop

Once you have been through this whole
process, and ended up changing the headsail
size, then you will need to change the lead
and sheet positions and retrim the headsail all
over again as described in Chapter 5. Then
you go back to trimming the mainsail afresh
to the new headsail trim, and so it goes on...
Alternatively you can get it close enough,
and put the kettle on.

Fine tune

But for those who have had enough tea, fine
tuning the trim can be very rewarding once you
get into it. Indeed the process of fine tuning to
get the boat in the `groove' with a slight weather
helm can be quite addictive. When you get a
gust or puff of wind you will get excessive
weather helm, so ease the traveller or the
mainsheet, whichever is easiest. When the wind
goes light again the rudder will lose its weather
helm, and feel 'soggy', so you pull the traveller
up and/or sheet on. But not too much; use the
leech telltale to tell you when to stop. Then wait
for the next gust. All the elements are
connected, and I hope I have shown here how
they can be used with and against each other.
Remember, it's all a question of balance; you
shouldn't have to fight the boat.

7 Heavy weather and shortening sail

Maintaining the balance of the boat is the priority when reducing sail area (shortening sail) in a strengthening wind. You must reduce the headsail and mainsail size in the right order to keep a reasonable amount of weather helm. If you can keep the helm balanced then you won't have to fight the boat to steer it. It is all too easy to make things much harder than they need be in heavy weather, if you unbalance the boat by reefing the wrong sails at the wrong time. The best way to see how this works is to imagine what happens onboard in a steadily building breeze.

A strengthening breeze

We have already seen how you need to ease the mainsheet a little in each gust of wind to balance the rudder. As the wind increases, each successive gust means easing more mainsheet to control the weather helm, until the main is continually backwinding. So you depower the headsail, by moving the lead position as we discussed in Chapter 6. But the wind keeps building, and eventually it won't be enough. Now the mainsail is flogging all the time and you have lee helm. The boat will be almost impossible to steer. You know you must shorten sail - but which sail first?

The answer is in the balance of the boat. With the mainsail flogging and the headsail still working, the centre of effort of the boat is too far forward. That's why you have lee helm, except for those few moments that you can sheet on the mainsail. You need to move the centre of effort back. That means either making the headsail less powerful, or making the mainsail more powerful.

In fact reducing the headsail size achieves both. The headsail becomes less powerful. But

Once the mainsail is flogging all the time, you will have lee helm because the headsail is the only sail that's working - pushing the centre of effort too far forward.

because the boat is no longer over-canvassed and the headsail is creating less backwind, you can now sheet the mainsail on again. Which is effectively powering up the mainsail and also moving the centre of effort back. The boat is in balance once more.

Mainsail reefed and headsail furled -
this yacht has shortened sail to keep
the helm nicely in balance.

1. Setting up to reef the mainsail. Attach the topping lift
to the end of the boom, and check the reefing line.

4. Once the halyard is tight and cleated,
wind in the reefing line.

At least until the wind cranks up another five
knots! Is it now time to reef the mainsail? Let the
boat tell you the answer: again think about the
balance. The rule is that if you can ease the main
enough to give the boat neutral or lee helm
before the mainsail is flogging, reduce the
headsail size again. But don't forget, every time
you reduce the headsail size, you must adjust
the lead position to keep the sail working
efficiently.

Eventually, the reduction in the headsail size
will shift the balance of the boat and even with
the main fully eased and flogging you will still
have significant weather helm. The centre of
effort is too far back. Now is the time to reef

the mainsail. This will move the centre of effort
forward.

If you follow these rules, you will shorten sail
comfortably with a balanced helm, right up to
storm jib and trysail. A balanced boat is one that
you don't have to fight. And when the weather is
bad you need all the help you can get.

Sail handling systems

How you actually go about shortening sail will
depend on which sail handling system your
yacht carries. The different systems that have
appeared in recent years have all increased the
cruising sailor's choice in performance, cost and

2. Ease the mainsheet and lower the halyard; the man at the mast then hooks in the reef at the new tack.

3. With the tack hooked up, raise the main halyard.

5. With the reefing line and halyard both tight, sheet the mainsail back on.

6. It only remains to take up the spare sail with a line around the boom.

ease of handling. Your willingness to go sailing at all, especially if you sail short-handed, will be affected by how easy it is to shorten sail when the wind gets up. But nothing comes for free, and as we will see optimising ease of handling can mean added cost and compromising on performance.

Mainsails

There are four principal choices in mainsail handling systems: conventional slab reefing, fully-battened, in-mast furling and in-boom furling.

Slab reefing

The traditional slab reefing system on a short-battened mainsail consists of additional holes and reinforcement patches that allow the sail to be lowered and the spare sail to be taken up and lashed to the boom. It has the advantage of being cheap and simple both to build and to maintain. All that's required in the way of hardware are the reefing lines at the clew end of the boom and a hook at the tack end. The sail has two or three sets of reinforced patches for the reef point tacks and clews on the luff and leech of the sail, and perhaps a set of holes running parallel to the boom between each set of tack and clew patches that allow the sail to be

This fully battened mainsail has been reefed with the help of lazy jacks which guide the mainsail onto the boom.

tied to the boom. The lack of any complex hardware gives this system its only real benefit, which is cost. The main disadvantage is in ease of handling.

Taking a reef in requires at least two people in addition to the helmsman, both of whom need a reasonable amount of strength and agility to work on the winches and at the mast. Preparation is the most important thing when reefing. Once you start, the flogging mainsail makes communication and co-ordination difficult. And the flogging breaks down sailcloth and snaps battens, so it's important to do the manoeuvre quickly. Sometime when you are in the dock, mark the halyard so you know exactly how far to lower it for each reef. Then when it comes to the reef itself, have all the relevant lines ready and ensure that everybody knows precisely what their job is; check that the topping lift is tensioned to keep the boom in the air once the halyard is eased; that the main halyard will ease smoothly and isn't knotted; that the reefing line is through the reefing point and

tied off to the boom properly. When you start the reef, lower the halyard and ease the mainsheet at the same time. Have someone stationed at the mast to hook the tack down - they then give the instruction to go back up on the halyard and to wind on the reefing line. Don't sheet the sail back on until both halyard and reefing line are tight, because it's impossible to get enough tension on with the sail filling.

Fully battened sails

The traditional system of short battens on the mainsail leech originally gave way to full length battens in certain types of racing boat for performance reasons. The full length batten allows the support of a much greater roach, which is the area of sail at the top of the leech. For aerodynamic reasons, a sail with a significant amount of roach and a 'fat' head (the famous Spitfire wing profile) is more efficient than one with the more traditional triangular shape and 'thin' head. Full length battens also hold and form the sail much more effectively

A mainsail reefed with the in-mast furling system.

between the lazy jack lines and on the boom.

The downsides to a fully-battened mainsail are the weight and the cost. The battens themselves add significantly to the weight of the sail. This can be offset to some extent by using lighter cloth, because of the strength the battens give the sail. A heavier and more complex mast track and car system is required to hoist a fully-battened sail. All this additional hardware and construction also adds significantly to the cost compared to a conventional slab reefing system and soft battened sail. Nevertheless, a fully-battened main has a better aerodynamic performance through the wind range than any other sail. It is also reasonably easy to use, though not quite so simple as in-mast furling.

In-mast furling

In-mast furling was developed by Ted Hood with his Stoway system. The mainsail rolls onto a furling rod mounted inside a special mast with an open back. The advantages to this system are in the ease of handling. The mainsail is reefed by winding it into the mast. You ease the mainsheet and outhaul as you go so that the sail luffs rather than flogs, and remains under tension. Sail area is quickly and widely adjustable. Unfortunately there are disadvantages in both cost and sailing performance. In-mast furling requires a brand-new mast section; it cannot be retro-fitted to your current mast because of the structural demands of the open back. So the cost of in-mast furling always includes the mast, which is also more expensive than a standard spar because of the additional engineering.

The performance disadvantages arise because the sail is rolled inside the mast, and you cannot fit conventional horizontal battens to the sail. This means the sail must be undersized, because there are no battens to support the roach. The leech is often made 'hollow' or concave for in-mast furling. The sail also lacks the structural and shape reinforcement that battens provide. Solutions to this problem include both vertical battens and air battens. The air battens are pumped up from an on-board compressor once the sail is unfurled. But both these solutions add

than short battens. You can let the solid battens do much of the work in shaping the sail, rather than rely on the design and loading of the cloth. But there are other benefits from full length battens, unconnected with performance, that have made them popular with cruising boats.

The rigidity that the battens impart to the sail significantly helps its durability. The battens make it harder for the sail to flog in the wind, which slows the breakdown of the cloth. It also makes the sail a great deal quieter and easier to handle. A fully-battened mainsail is slab-reefed in exactly the same way as a traditional one, but the battens control the mainsail during the process, stopping it flogging and holding it parallel to the boom so that it is much easier to gather. The addition of lazy jacks (two or three lines running from the mast to the boom parallel to the leech) means the sail is gathered as it is lowered and makes the process easier still. They can also be used with short battened sails, but they work better with full length battens because the battens guarantee the sail stays

Returning home from a stormy passage under storm jib and trysail.

to the cost. There are also problems in shaping the sail, because it has to be rolled flat round a rod; these are dealt with under roller furling headsails, below. In addition, the mast is wider in section than a normal spar, which reduces the aerodynamic efficiency of the mainsail. And finally the mast weighs more than a conventional spar.

Nevertheless, if safety and ease of handling are your concerns, in-mast furling is the ultimate solution. If you can afford it these qualities may easily outweigh the loss of performance to those who regularly cruise short-handed or long distance.

In-boom furling

This is a variation on in-mast furling where the sail is rolled into the boom rather than the mast. Theory would indicate some advantages for this system over in-mast furling. The sail can still use horizontal battens, which give it a better shape. The additional weight of the furling gear is in the boom rather than aloft in the mast. And keeping the weight low gives a less damaging increase in pitching. On the cost side, changing to in-boom furling doesn't require the purchase of a new mast. But the practical aspects make it difficult for the system to work properly. While the mast had to be wider to allow it to hold the vertically-rolled mainsail, rolling the sail horizontally gives an even greater problem if it is to fit inside the boom. It is not easy to engineer such a boom, with strong enough vang and mainsheet take-off points, to a reasonable size and weight. There is also the problem of keeping tension on the foot as the sail is rolled. That's not to say these problems can't be solved with high quality engineering. But you should pay more attention to these details of the design before purchasing an in-boom system, compared with the more widely successful concept of in-mast furling.

Trysails

The storm trysail is a separate sail to the mainsail, and it is designed to balance the boat and provide windward sailing ability in the worst conditions. Many people carry trysails in the bilge. For anything more than day sailing in inshore waters, that's a minimum requirement. But those who are more serious about their cruising and undertake passages of more than a couple of days, particularly short-handed, should also consider the proper preparation of the storm trysail.

The trysail is designed to be hoisted on slides on its own separate luff groove. This luff groove should run down the mast beside the mainsail luff groove, but extend past the gooseneck to the deck. Before departing, the trysail is attached to the groove by slides, then folded into a bag and tied to the deck at the base of the mast. Ideally the sheeting system is fixed to the clew of the trysail, and includes a snap shackle that allows it to be attached to the appropriate fixed point aft in the boat. This is then carried in the bag as well. You can find the right place for the sheet lead position by hoisting the sail on a normal day. The spinnaker sheet pad-eye is often about right, or a stern mooring cleat. If there isn't anything appropriate already fitted,

This headsail is hanked directly to the wire headstay, ready to hoist.

A headsail set up and ready to hoist in a headstay foil.

you should add it to the deck gear.

The trysail is then ready for a simple, safe hoist. The mainsail is dropped to the deck, still attached to the mast and lashed to the boom. The boom is then lashed to the deck so the whole unit is safely locked in place. The trysail can now be pulled out of the bag. The sheeting system is snapped to the appropriate point, and the sail hoisted on the main halyard. The important points about this system are that you don't have to clear the mainsail off the mast and boom - which can be highly dangerous or impossible in some conditions; the trysail is ready to be hoisted with a minimum of effort; and the sail can be hoisted without the boom - much safer generally in extreme conditions, but also vital when the boom is broken. The trysail is built without battens and with a hollow leech, designed to take the worst possible weather. In conjunction with a storm jib it provides the all-important balanced sail plan that we talked about earlier. It gives the boat windward ability - so necessary to get you out of trouble when there is no sea room to leeward.

Headsails

The choices are simpler for headsails, partly because there are only two main options and because the ease of use of roller reefing systems is not compromised by high extra cost.

Hanked or headstay foils

The simplest way, at least in principle, of reducing headsail area is to take the big one down and put a smaller sail up instead. Hanked or luff groove headstay foil systems both work this way. The hanked sail clips directly to the wire headstay. The headstay foil is fitted over the top of the wire headstay and it provides a grooved track, like the mainsail luff track, that the bolt rope in the headsail luff slides up. The first system is more secure, the sail being attached to the boat even when it is lowered, but changing sails is a slow process. The advantage of both is that each separate sail that the yacht carries can be precisely designed and engineered to the conditions in which it is hoisted. The downside, of course, is that to change the sail you have to take one off and put the other on. That involves someone on the foredeck and someone at the mast or in the cockpit.

Roller reefing

Roller reefing works by rolling the headsail onto the headstay to reduce its area. There is usually a drum at both the head and the tack, the sail being attached to the headstay through a luff groove like that described above. The roller reefing control line can be run back into the cockpit. That means that shortening sail no longer requires any heroics on the foredeck. The advantages in ease of use are clear. And, since you now only require one sail through most of the wind range, the additional cost of the roller reefing hardware can be offset by the need for fewer sails.

The only disadvantage is probably that which is of least concern to the cruising person - sailing performance. The requirements of the furling system and the yacht's sailing needs are in complete conflict. The best shape for rolling onto the headstay is a completely flat sail with no built-in shape at all. That is also the worst solution aerodynamically. We must also consider the sail area that remains when the sail is only partially furled. This must continue to perform effectively both structurally and aerodynamically. The biggest problem when you furl a headsail is that the middle of the sail is where most of the depth is. So as you roll it up the sail becomes proportionally fuller. That is exactly the opposite to what is required as the wind increases. The second problem is that the major loads in the sail run up the edges from the corners. As you roll the sail the corners move up the leech, luff and foot. This transfers the major loads into new areas of cloth. The simplest solution is to make the sail out of heavyweight cloth throughout. But this also makes the whole sail heavier and more expensive than it need be, unduly reducing its performance in light airs. And we are trying to make one sail efficient through the entire wind range!

These problems can be dealt with to a large

A headsail roller reefing drum. The wire control line is running aft on the port side.

extent by good construction and design, particularly through use of the tri-radial panel layout. Because the panels radiate out of the clew, head and tack the load is kept on the same panels all the way through the furl. This allows the sail to be both light and strong. (This is in comparison to cross cut sails, where the panels in the middle of the sail become loaded when the sail is half furled. So they have to be much heavier than is otherwise necessary.) The problem of the sail getting fuller through the furl is helped by the addition of a shaped foam strip down the luff. This is designed to compensate for the thicker cloth at the corners and the greater shape in the middle. It allows the headsail to roll more evenly and smoothly along its length, and flattens the sail through the furl. Finally the radial layouts make it easy to add a

The shaped foam strip down the luff of this roller furling headsail is designed to help the sail keep its shape when it is reefed.

This is what happens without the foam strip - a bundle of extra cloth makes the sail very deep in the front and middle - just what you don't want. You can also see the strain on the cross-cut panels at the tack and head. Radial panels would be aligned to take this strain. The darker strip is the sacrificial sunstrip

sacrificial sunstrip on the leech and foot panels. This is the only part of the sail that is exposed when the sail is furled. If you do leave the sail rigged and furled for long periods of time it is only the sunstrip that suffers from the weather. It is a lot cheaper to replace the sunstrip than the whole sail!

We have already looked at the principles of helm balance that can be used to decide when to furl the headsail and by how much. But there are a few more points about the mechanics of the operation that are worth making. The first is that as you roll up the headsail you will be moving the position of the clew in relation to the sheet lead position. This means that you will have to check the telltales to reset the lead position

when you furl the headsail. Unfortunately, if you have a single telltale at each height, the chances are that it will disappear into the rolled headsail as soon as you furl up some sail. So you should have a couple of extra sets of telltales across the sail, so that there are always some visible.

One thing that will make this process simpler is marking the foot of the sail at the three or four specific points to which you normally furl it. Then you can use the telltales to find the right lead position for each reef. Once you have the correct lead position, you can mark the headsail

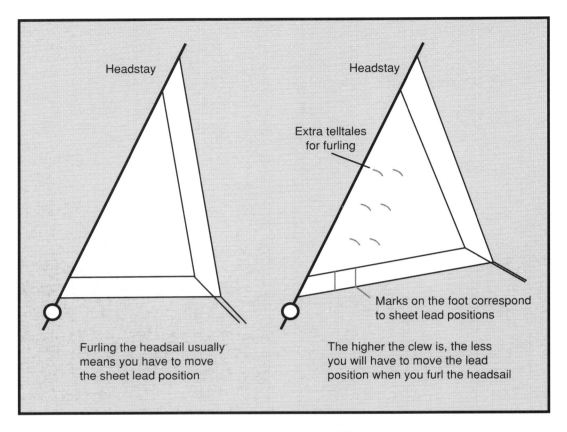

Headstay

Headstay

Extra telltales
for furling

Marks on the foot correspond
to sheet lead positions

Furling the headsail usually
means you have to move
the sheet lead position

The higher the clew is, the less
you will have to move the lead
position when you furl the headsail

lead track as well. With both track and sail marked, it will be much quicker to furl the sail in the future. Just roll up the sail, push the lead forward to the right mark - and off you go again.

There is a further trade-off here between ease of use and performance. The greater the distance between the clew of the sail and the deck, the shorter the distance that you will have to move the lead position when you furl the headsail. But by making the sail with a high clew, there is a loss of aerodynamic efficiency. Which is why you will always see racing boats with headsails that come right down onto the deck. But most cruising people seem happy to trade the small loss of performance for the extra convenience of the high clew. An additional advantage is that it keeps the foot of the sail out of the water when you are reaching. So when you buy a headsail for roller furling, you should check whether the sailmaker intends to cut it with a high clew or not - and ask for it if you want it.

Storm jibs

The storm jib, which like the storm trysail spends much of its life in the bilge with the owner hoping it will never be needed, has become more important with the widespread use of the roller reefing headsail. The reason is that the roller reefing headsail is often attached to the headstay through the bolt rope and a luff groove. Should you have a problem with the sail and wish to hoist a replacement, you have to remove the sail from the groove. Once out of the groove the sail is all too easily washed off the foredeck if there aren't sufficient hands available to keep it there. This is in contrast to a hanked sail, which can be lowered and left attached while the replacement is hanked on and hoisted above it. There are also problems in the use of highly reefed roller headsails in extreme conditions. While a sail can be designed and built to perform in a very wide wind range, a sail that will be used in 5 knots cannot be rolled up

The storm jib has been hoisted on the inner forestay, the roller furling headsail having been safely furled away. You can also see how the mainsail is kept safely lashed on the boom while the trysail is hoisted.

to cope with 50 knots. Even if the construction is strong enough, there is so much sail wrapped round the headstay and the sail area has moved so far forward, that the boat is unlikely to be able to sail upwind. With all the headsail area at the headstay the bow will be blown downwind and you won't be able to hoist enough mainsail area to balance the lee helm. As with the storm trysail, a storm jib is there to provide balanced sail area in extreme conditions.

Anyone who goes far enough offshore to run any risk of seeing these conditions should consider carrying a separately-hoistable storm jib. This is set on an inner forestay, which is a second headstay, often removeable for day sailing. Adding this system to your boat may require strengthening both the mast and the deck. The storm jib can be hanked on to this stay prior to departure. It is bagged up with the sheets attached in exactly the same way as the storm trysail. Then if the worst does happen and you lose or fully furl the normal headsail, the storm jib is easily hoisted. It is designed to work in extreme conditions. Because it is set on the inner forestay the sail is further back in the boat, which helps enormously in balancing the helm and allowing you to claw your way upwind - perhaps off a rocky lee shore.

8 Light air sailing

So far we have used the balance of the helm to set up the sail trim. But what happens in light air when, even with full sail up, the helm becomes 'soggy'? Soggy's not perhaps the most technical phrase, but it does describe that feeling when the tiller or wheel has neither lee nor weather helm, and you have to push it around to make the rudder work at all. The boat is bobbing about and the sails are probably flapping from side to side, unable to fill properly. What can we do to get her moving? Well, you could turn the engine on, which is probably the response of most people to these circumstances. But if you've got plenty of time, and you don't want the peace of the day shattered by the diesel, sailing in light airs can be very pleasant.

The boat will be at its most responsive in light air when you are sailing upwind or close reaching. Having the wind on or aft of the beam feels terrible in light airs because what little speed you do generate takes you away from the wind. There is no breeze travelling over the deck at all, and you feel becalmed. In fact it is common for racing yachts to 'over-run' the breeze in these conditions - to sail faster than the wind, and have the sails go aback! In contrast, sailing upwind builds the apparent wind across the deck, and makes you feel you're getting somewhere. So if you want to sail in light winds, I'd recommend you stick to trying to go upwind or close to it!

Sail shape when you're drifting

The first thing is to try and get the sail shape right. In very light air, when there's barely a ripple on the water and flags are struggling to stir themselves, the rule is to keep the boat moving and keep the sails working. In these conditions you will find it difficult to get the boat moving on anything other than a tight reaching angle. Try to go too close upwind, or too far

Sails set up flat and twisted for drifting along on a reach. The topping lift is being used to raise the boom and keep the mainsail leech open.

downwind and the boat will stop. Only experimentation will find this angle for your boat. But you can start by keeping the apparent wind (the wind you feel on your face and see on the burgee) at about thirty to forty degrees off the bow. You also need to have a 'forgiving' sail shape, with the sails as flat and twisted as possible. It is less work for the wind to follow a flat, twisted shape, than to follow a full one with a tight leech: the fragile flow over the sail is less likely to stall and break down. This keeps the sail working, generating lift and forward motion for the yacht.

Mainsail

To flatten the mainsail pull the outhaul on tight. If you can bend the mast with either the topmast or running backstay, then that will also help flatten the sail. Getting the sail to twist is more difficult, as the weight of the boom is often enough to close the leech. Certainly the vang should be completely loose. Pull the traveller to windward as far as possible, so that the mainsheet pulls sideways on the boom rather than down. The hope is that you will get the top batten telltale flying all the time - if there is enough wind to get it to fly at all! Often there isn't and the weight of the boom tightens the leech however you set up the vang, traveller and mainsheet. In these cases you can cheat a little by attaching the topping lift to the end of the boom, then pulling it up to take the weight of the boom off the sail and so free up the leech.

(Above) To get the headsail leech eased and twisted, the weight of the sheet is taken by the crewman, holding the clew by hand - but this is perhaps a little too keen!

(Below) With a little more wind the outhaul can be eased to make the mainsail fuller and more powerful. You don't need the topping lift to get the leech telltales to fly, either.

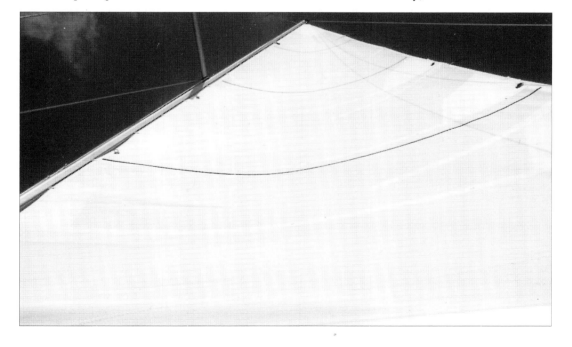

Headsail

The story with the headsail is much the same, except that you do not have the weight of the boom to contend with. The telltales won't be much help in this really light stuff, as they will be struggling to fly. To get the headsail flat pull the lead position aft until the sail is sheeted more along the foot than is normal. This flattens the base of the sail and eases the leech. But don't sheet too tight to try to flatten the sail too much as this just makes the angle of attack very narrow. Remember, you are trying to sail on a close reach to maintain any speed that you can generate, so the jib can afford to be a little eased to help you sail at this angle. The halyard should be snug enough to take up creases in the luff, but no more - unless the sail is old and the draft further aft than 50%.

A little more wind

With winds between 3 knots and 8 knots the sails can slowly be made fuller, because they are more able to generate power in the building breeze. And as they become fuller they can be sheeted on tighter, and the leech twist removed.

Mainsail

Even at eight knots you still shouldn't need to pull on any cunningham, unless your sail is very old and the draft goes backwards at the first sign of any pressure in the sail! But you can ease the outhaul progressively as the wind increases to eight knots to give the bottom of the sail some shape. At eight knots the outhaul is eased so that the last ten inches of the bottom batten point slightly to windward. You still won't need to take up the vang at all. But you should be able to let off the topping lift and play the mainsheet. You should be able to keep the traveller to windward until eight knots without getting too much weather helm. The idea is just to play the mainsheet according to the top batten telltale. At three knots you are still aiming to get that top telltale flying all the time. By five knots you can maybe even sheet on a little more to stall it out deliberately ten percent of the time. In flat water at eight knots you can sheet on hard enough to stall the telltale fifty percent of the time. If the

Enough wind for the headsail to support itself and the telltales to fly. The lead position is all the way aft, and the sail is powered up just the right amount.

water is bumpy aim for it to be flying eighty percent of the time.

Headsail

With the headsail the important cross-over is when there is enough wind to start using the telltales properly. Then you can start trimming according to the rules in Chapter 5. This will be somewhere around five or six knots, about the same time that the leech telltale starts flying happily. Until that point you are still working at keeping a flat and twisted shape, as we described above. It is important to keep the lead inboard. Moving it outboard reduces the power from the sail enormously.

Other tricks

Use the crew weight to heel the boat to leeward. This helps the sails 'fall' into shape and allows the air to spend more energy on moving the

Light air sailing is a good opportunity to stare at the scenery and reflect on life! Sitting to leeward to do it helps the sails fall into shape.

boat forward, and less on holding the sail shape. It will also help to make the helm feel less soggy. The asymmetric shape of the heeled-over hull forces the yacht to turn. When the mast tip is heeled to leeward, the boat wants to turn into the wind - which gives you weather helm. When the mast tip is heeled to windward, the boat wants to turn away from the wind - which gives you lee helm. So heeling the boat to leeward in light air gives you a little of the weather helm that the wind is refusing to provide! Incidentally, dinghy sailors use this to help steer the boat round corners. By heeling the dinghy to windward, for instance, they help it bear away. And the less rudder they use, the less of a brake is applied to the boat through the turn.

Although it is against the racing rules, there is nothing unseamanlike for a cruising boat to use moveable weight to help achieve the leeward

heel. You can pile any spare sails down to leeward on the cabin floor, as well as the lunch box, the beer crates or anything else that's easily shifted.

Another technique is to keep the weight low when there are bad waves or a nasty choppy seaway. The idea is that the lower you keep the centre of gravity, the less the boat will pitch and slow down in the waves. Taken to an extreme, as racing boats are inclined to do, this can mean two thirds of the crew sitting on the keel for the entire day, slowly chewing their way through the menu. I've finished more than one long, light air race absolutely starving, only to find that there's not a single edible item left on the entire boat! But the attraction of sitting on the keel of a cruising boat in light air and a bad swell is limited to the times when it's pouring with rain. And by then I reckon most of us have the engine on!!

9 Downwind sailing

Downwind sailing starts when the wind first blows aft of the beam, and continues until you are running dead before the wind. Running dead downwind is something of a special case in sail trim. Remember the flat plate that we turned square to the wind? It was pushed straight backwards, creating all drag and no lift. That's exactly what your sails need to do to push you dead downwind. Their job is purely to project as much area as possible which gets in the way of the wind flow to create drag - there is no need for any lift. But as soon as you want to travel across the wind flow - in other words you want to start broad or beam reaching - you will need more than just drag from your sails taking you in the direction of the wind. You will require lift to push you forward across the wind and your sails will need to be more efficient foils. We will look in turn at trimming the mainsail and headsail for each of these two cases in turn.

Trimming on a reach

The rules we established for trimming the mainsail and headsail off the wind in Chapters 5 and 6 are exactly the same for reaching downwind. But there are a couple of additional points we can make.

Mainsail

It is important to make the mainsail shape much fuller as you turn further off the wind. Do this by easing the outhaul progressively: when you are broad reaching it should be about six inches looser than the normal upwind position. Also loosen off any cunningham that you have applied, or drop the halyard two inches if you don't have a cunningham. This is all to make the sail as powerful as possible. Once the wind is aft of the beam it does not have the same heeling effect as when you are close reaching with the wind forward of the beam, so you can set the sails up to be fuller and more powerful.

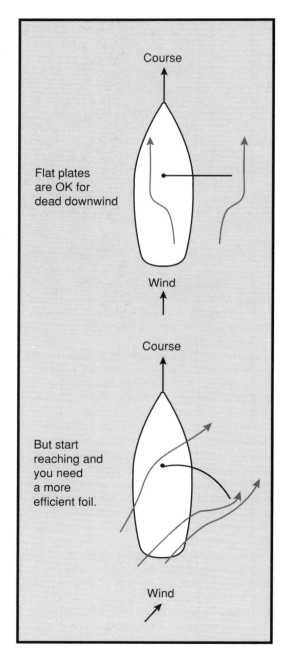

Course

Flat plates are OK for dead downwind

Wind

Course

But start reaching and you need a more efficient foil.

Wind

Once you are sailing dead downwind, the headsail becomes blanketed by the mainsail, and will not work.

Goose-winging the headsail with the spinnaker pole. You can just see that the tell-tales are working backwards, showing the reversed flow across the sail.

Headsail

The headsail becomes progressively less effective as you turn from beam reaching to a broad reach. It slowly becomes blanketed and trapped in the lee of the mainsail. There are two ways to maintain efficiency: you can drop the headsail and hoist a spinnaker, which we will cover in the next chapter; or you can goose-wing the headsail.

Goose-winging the headsail means pulling it across to the windward side with a sheet, and holding it out there using a pole attached to the mast and the headsail clew. This could be the spinnaker pole or a whisker pole, which some boats will have for just this purpose. Although a lot of people only try it when they are running

dead downwind, it is possible to make goose-winging work when you are broad reaching by reversing the flow across the headsail. (Then the wind flows from the leech to the luff.) This takes a bit of practice though. It is easy to sail too high and have the headsail try to blow back across the boat. Or to sail too low to keep the headsail filling, and end up somewhere other than where you want to go!

Trimming dead downwind

As you continue to bear away from a broad reach onto a run your sails must start working as flat plates. The idea is to make them project the maximum area in the way of the wind by making your sails as 'big' as possible. But a second and more important point is that dead downwind is

Although the mainsail leech has been kept tight, the headsail is very open and twisted at the top - that's what's causing the rolling!

the most dangerous point of sailing, because of the risk of an accidental gybe. It is easy to start 'running by the lee' - with the wind blowing from the same side of the boat that the mainsail is on. Then it only takes a slight change in wind direction, or a wave rolling the boat, and the wind can get behind the mainsail and fling it across the deck - along with anyone standing in the way. Not too much of a problem in six knots, but a major hazard in twenty. Sail trim in these conditions needs to be as much about safety as it does about speed. It is a point of sail to be avoided by the prudent mariner whenever possible - but for those in a hurry or in search of excitement, here are some thoughts.

Mainsail

We must get the mainsail flat, which means pulling out on the outhaul as hard as possible. We must also keep the leech tight. The biggest danger running dead downwind in a breeze is the aptly named 'death roll'. If the leech of the sail is too loose, it allows the top of the sail to twist round past ninety degrees to the boat. Then it starts pushing the masthead sideways rather than forwards which begins the rolling motion that can end in an accidental gybe. So keep the leech of the sail tight. Leaving the cunningham off will help. The vang is more important. If you keep the vang tight, you will stop the top of the mainsail twisting. And don't ease the main out too far. Doing so makes it more likely that the top of the sail will push sideways rather than forwards, encouraging the rolling.

You can also rig a preventer. This is a rope led from the vang attachment on the boom to the leeward rail. It holds the boom out to leeward, and stops it gybing. However, it won't stop the yacht broaching to windward if you do let the roll get out of control. Then the main is held in the air, trapping the boat on its side. So always make sure that the preventer is led to a winch, is long enough to let the boom slowly back across the boat and has enough turns on the winch to keep it under control.

If the boat does start to roll, or if it feels scary or out of control, head up towards a broad or even a beam reach and sheet on the mainsail immediately. This is another occasion when you will need someone manning the preventer: he will need to ease it to allow you to sheet on the main. The boat will not roll on a beam reach, when the wind is trying to push her over to leeward. She will only roll when the wind is blowing onto the stern, when bad sail trim can allow it to push the boat first to leeward, then to windward. And always make sure people are alert and keep their heads down in these circumstances, just in case.

Here the pole is keeping the leech tight and the clew low. This will stop the 'death roll' starting.

Headsail

The headsail is ineffective downwind if it is on the same side as the mainsail. It just sits in the lee of the mainsail and flaps uselessly. For the headsail to be effective you need to goose-wing it as we discussed above. Once you are goose-winged you need to be careful that the headsail only pushes the boat forwards, not sideways. This, as with the mainsail, can start the yacht rolling. The roll starts accidentally with a goose-winged headsail by having the pole too high or the sheet too loose. Both of these allow the leech to twist off and start pushing the masthead sideways - beginning the death roll. So if you are goose-winging the headsail in anything more than fifteen knots of wind keep the sheet tight. And set the pole low so that the leech is not twisted.

10 Spinnakers and cruising chutes

Spinnakers have always had a bad press and to some extent it's deserved. Since you only have limited control over the clew and the tack, the free floating nature of the spinnaker can endow it with what seems at times like free will. Fortunately, there is no stimulus when we're cruising to fly the sail in anything other than safe conditions - which is more than can be said for the attitude in some racing boats! And the recent development of the cruising chute and launch systems like the snuffer have provided us with an alternative downwind sail that is a great deal better behaved.

Trimming the cruising chute

The cruising chute is set from the bow of the boat, much like a genoa, except that it is not usually attached to the headstay. If you tried to sail dead downwind with the cruising chute it

Set the cruising chute with the tack just above the pulpit.

The lead position is set almost as far aft as it can go, to allow the leech to open. The sheet is still safely under the boom.

would be in the lee of the mainsail, where it would be as inefficient as the headsail in similar circumstances. But, like a headsail, the cruising chute starts working properly when you start reaching. The only adjustment that is normally available is trimming the sheet and possibly moving the sheet lead position. If the height of the tack can be varied then it should always be set before the hoist at just above the pulpit, but most systems have a fixed tack strop. If you're not sure how to set the cruising chute, or the spinnaker for that matter, this is covered in Chapter 11. If the sheet lead position has not been determined by where the boatbuilder placed the block, then set the lead as far outboard and as far aft as you can get it. The only thing you have to be careful of is whether the sheet can flick over the boom when the sail is flogging. If this happens, drop the sail and

move the sheet lead forward a couple of feet before you try again.

For the cruising chute to work you must be sailing on a broad reach or closer to the wind. This means that the air will be flowing across the chute, as with a headsail or mainsail. Trimming the sheet of the cruising chute is very much like trimming a headsail. If you put telltales on the luff they will help you trim it, just as they help you trim a headsail. But telltales are not as essential as they are for a headsail because the sail is made from a lighter cloth. This is more responsive and so the luff lifts or curls more easily. The luff curling means the same thing as the windward telltale lifting: it is a sign that you need to sheet the sail a little tighter, or bear away a little bit.

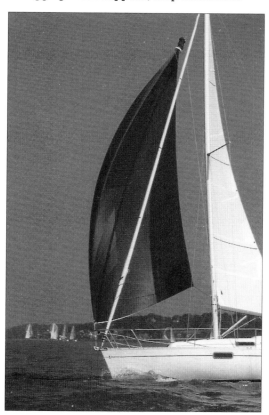

Ease the sheet until the luff is just on the point of curling, as it is here.

If you bear away too much and try to sail dead downwind with the cruising chute it will flog in the lee of the mainsail - just as the headsail would.

The cruising chute is at its most efficient when the luff is just curling. If you are sailing a course you will go fastest if you keep retrimming the sheet to this point. So ease the sheet until the luff curls, then sheet back on a touch, then ease it again and so on. Alternatively, you can cleat the sheet and steer to the sail. The rule then is to keep heading up very gently until the luff of the sail curls, then bear away a little. This will keep the sail working efficiently.

One danger with steering to the curl of the luff is that it is possible to bear away too far, so that the cruising spinnaker gets blanketed behind the mainsail and collapses. The first sign of this can be the luff curling as it starts to collapse - but if you bear away more, you'll only make it worse! Telltales will help you in this situation. When you first start to bear away too much the leeward telltale will droop, even though the sail will still be set and full at that point. You must now ease the sheet or head up to get it flying again. Remember that, because cruising chutes don't

work dead downwind; if you keep easing the sheet and bearing away the sail will eventually become blanketed and will collapse.

Trimming the spinnaker

The symmetric spinnaker is a more flexible sail than the cruising chute because the tack is set from a spinnaker pole. This means the sail can work dead downwind, because you can get it clear of the mainsail by pulling the pole aft. But it will also work on a reach, by letting the pole forward towards the headstay. The flexibility is a result of the free-flying nature of the sail - and so is its bad reputation. Unlike headsails and mainsails none of the edges is fixed to a spar or headstay. And unlike the cruising chute the tack is almost infinitely adjustable through the spinnaker pole. Although this means it is possible to trim the spinnaker into a vast range of shapes, these can be wrong as well as right. And in some circumstances, such as strong winds and downwind sailing, they can also be

The trimmer is about to ease the sheet, to see where the luff starts curling.

The luff is now curling, but although the trimmer doesn't know it yet, he has eased the sheet too far and the spinnaker is just about to collapse.

Just like that!

The spinnaker trimmed for a broad reach. The tack and clew are level, the pole is parallel to the deck and roughly in line with the boom. The sheet is then eased until the luff is just about to curl.

▸ get the spinnaker flying again ▸se the pole forward a couple of ▸t and pull on the sheet.

The helmsman also bears away twenty degrees - check the bow against the land.

Once the spinnaker is flying, you can start to pull the pole back and ease the sheet out again.

The spinnaker trimmed for a beam reach, with the pole held off the headstay by the guy. Although you will not be able to keep the boom and pole in line any longer, the pole is still parallel to the deck and the tack and clew are still level.

dangerous. The spinnaker is definitely not a sail for beginners.

We'll concentrate on some simple pointers that will allow you to fly the sail safely on a broad reach. Hoist the sail on a broad reach (see Chapter 11), and once it is set use the topping lift to adjust the outboard end of the pole so that the tack is the same height as the leeward clew. If the inboard end of the pole is adjustable, set it so that the pole is parallel to the deck. Check the mainsail trim: ease it out until the luff is just lifting, then sheet on a touch. Now pull the spinnaker pole back with the guy, so that it is approximately in a straight line with the boom. Now all your adjustment goes into the sheet, and the job is similar to trimming the cruising chute: keep easing the sheet until the luff is just curling, then trim it back on a foot. Or you can cleat the sheet and sail to the spinnaker luff just as you sail to the cruising chute luff. If the sail does collapse you will need to do three things; ease the pole forward a foot, bear away ten or twenty degrees and sheet on. Once the sail is full, go back through the trimming process above.

If you wish to sail closer to the wind you will have to let the pole go forward towards the headstay by easing the guy. You must sheet on as the pole goes forward, otherwise the luff will curl and the sail will collapse. As you do so you will also be sheeting the mainsail on. Keeping the boom and the pole in line is a good rule until you are beam reaching. Then you will need to let the pole right forward almost to the headstay, even though the mainsail is not on the centreline. Never let the pole rest on the headstay or you will break it. Although for most of us, beam reaching with a spinnaker is far too much like hard work. I'd recommend that you change to the headsail before this point.

And the same goes for sailing further off the wind than a broad reach. We have already issued warnings about the perils of sailing dead downwind, and doing so with the spinnaker is not going to make things any safer!

Velocity made good (VMG)

Velocity Made Good is a simple enough idea and is particularly valuable when passage

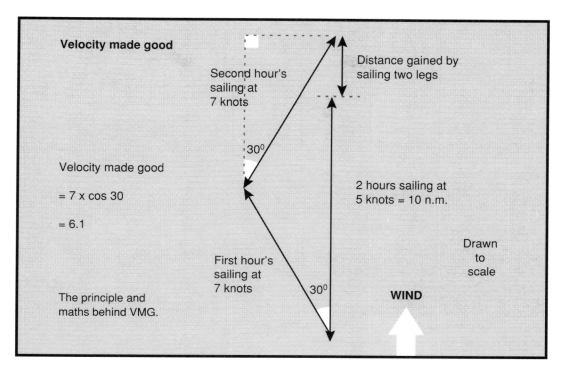

Velocity made good

Second hour's sailing at 7 knots

Distance gained by sailing two legs

30^0

Velocity made good

$= 7 \times \cos 30$

$= 6.1$

2 hours sailing at 5 knots = 10 n.m.

Drawn to scale

First hour's sailing at 7 knots

30^0

WIND

The principle and maths behind VMG.

sailing with a cruising chute. In fact you probably already understand the principle even if you've never heard the phrase before. Imagine that your destination lies dead downwind. You ease the main and sail straight towards it. Your boatspeed is 5 knots.

Now head up a little, to a true wind angle of 150 degrees, so that you are sailing 30 degrees above the rhumb line course. The boatspeed will increase, say to 7 knots. (It's true of most yachts that they sail faster broad reaching than they do dead running. This is even more likely to be the case when you are carrying a cruising chute or a spinnaker.)

So you have two choices, you can sail straight at the destination at 5 knots. Or you can sail thirty degrees high on one gybe for half the leg, then gybe over and sail thirty degrees high on the other gybe for the other half of the leg - all the while sailing at 7 knots. The question is, does the extra speed make up for the extra distance you are sailing, and get you there quicker?

VMG is the answer to the question - velocity made good in the direction of the course. VMG is calculated from the formula:

$$VMG = boatspeed \times \frac{cosine\ of\ the}{off\text{-}course\ angle.}$$

Which in this case means that sailing straight to the destination has a VMG of 5 knots, and sailing thirty degrees high has a VMG of 6.1 knots - over 1 knot quicker! By sailing further you get there faster. And all you need to calculate which is the more efficient sailing angle is a log or boatspeed meter, and a cosine table or calculator.

The other major advantage of VMG is that cruising spinnakers are designed for broad reaching. It is not only safer to hoist the cruising chute and sail on a broad reach (rather than trying to sail dead downwind to your destination, with or without a symmetrical spinnaker) it can also be quicker. The cruising chute gives you the extra speed that you need for a faster Velocity Made Good to your destination.

11 Hoists and drops

Getting spinnakers and cruising chutes up and down is the source of many people's nervousness about the sails. We will look at safe methods of hoisting and lowering the cruising chute using a sock, and the symmetric spinnaker using 'stops'.

Hoisting the cruising chute

The sock is a long tube of sailcloth that pulls down over the full length of the spinnaker from the head to the foot - bundling the sail into a long snake. The head appears out of the top, and the clews poke out of the bottom. So instead of hoisting yards of flogging sailcloth, the sock or 'snuffer' keeps it bundled up tight until the sail is fully hoisted. Although the sock can be used with both a cruising chute and a symmetric spinnaker, its use with the cruising chute provides the simplest of all downwind sail handling systems. It is particularly suited to those sailing short-handed and long distance. Exactly the same principles apply should you wish to use it with a symmetric spinnaker.

Preparation is everything in spinnaker work, and it starts with packing the chute properly. The easiest way to pack the sail is choose a day when there is no wind, and do it when in the marina or anchored. First push the head of the chute through the sock and fasten it. Make sure that the sock control line is not fouled or twisted round the head. Run down the leech and the luff, from the head down to the tack and from the head to the clew to check that the sail is not twisted. Then hoist the head on a halyard, pulling the sock down as the head goes up. Leave the tack and clew visible and poking out of the ends of the sock, so that you can find them easily to attach to the tack strop and the sheets when you need to. If the luff is longer than the leech, you will need to add a rope extension to the clew so that this pokes out of the foot of the sock. Once packed, the sock and chute can be

Pack the cruising chute by pushing the head through the sock until it reaches the top.

lowered again and kept below safely until needed.

Once you are out on the water and want to hoist the cruising chute, first furl the headsail. Fasten the tack to the headstay base or the headsail tack fitting using a rope strop to ensure that the tack will be clear above the pulpit. Fasten the sheet to the clew and run it aft to the lead at the back of the boat, making sure that it is outboard of all rigging and stanchions, and then onto a winch. Clip the halyard to the head of the sail. The sail can now be hoisted. The tighter the sock and the sail are pulled between the tack fitting and the halyard, the easier it will be to pull the sock up and off the sail. You must also make sure that there is enough room at the top of the mast for the gathered sock when it is pulled off the

The head of the chute is shackled to the top of the sock with a short wire strop. Check that the control line (bottom) is not twisted round the head.

Then clip the head to a halyard and hoist it. Separate the leech and the luff to make sure there are no twists, and pull the sock all the way down over the chute as it rises.

The tack of the cruising chute set up ready to go. Here we have fastened the tack strop to the bow roller. The height is set to keep the tack just above the pulpit. The sheet is run aft to the lead and then onto a winch. The sail is then hoisted to the top of the mast.

All that remains is to raise the sock using the control line, while someone else pulls on the sheet to help fill the sail. The wind will help you pull the sock up the sail.

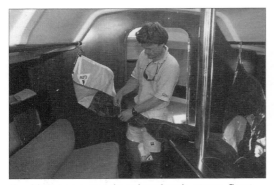

Packing a symmetric spinnaker in stops. Start at the head and each of the clews in turn and roll the spinnaker from one edge towards the other. Then tie it in the roll using a short length of wool. You should work down from the head first, to about two thirds the height of the sail. Then work in from each clew evenly.

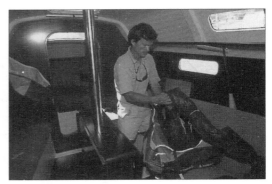

With the spinnaker stopped up, pack it in a bag. The square style of bag is best as it allows you to keep the head and clews separated. Start from the middle of the foot, working towards all three corners at once and fold the sail into the bag evenly. Keep the clews at the ends, and the head in the middle to ensure they do not become twisted. A good bag design will have Velcro fasteners that keep the three corners in place.

sail. To have the right tension and enough space for the sock you must ensure that the sailmaker builds the sail with a luff length that is short enough.

When you are all ready to set the chute, make sure you are on a broad reach, then pull on the sock control line to hoist it and free the spinnaker. If you sheet on as the sail gradually becomes free it will start to fill and this will help push the sock to the masthead. If any lines are fouled and the sock refuses to rise it is always best to lower the chute and clear the problem with it on the deck. The other reason that chutes can be obstinate in freeing themselves from the sock is that the cloth is old and perhaps wet. This vastly increases the friction between the sail and the sock compared to when the sail is new and has a shiny finish. If it becomes impossible to use the sock the only way to cure it may well be to buy a new sail!

Lowering the cruising chute

Lowering the cruising chute and sock is a reversal of the above process. Make sure you are on a broad reach, then ease the sheet until the sail collapses as you pull the sock back down over it. Once the chute is safely tucked back up in its sock, the whole thing can be lowered to the deck and detached.

Hoisting the symmetric spinnaker

Preparation is even more important when hoisting the symmetric spinnaker as there is more to go wrong. We are going to use a system called `stops'. These are wool ties that hold the spinnaker together while it is hoisted. When the sail is at the masthead, pulling on the sheet and guy starts to break the wool stops and the wind does the rest, filling the sail. Like the sock, it allows you to get the sail hoisted before it fills. So roll the spinnaker from leech to leech, working from the head down to about two thirds the height of the sail, and tie it in the roll with a couple of wraps of wool. You can do the same thing from both clews, rolling both the leeches to the foot. The windier it is, the more sail you need to stop up; about six feet from each corner is reasonable for light to medium air. But if you overdo it, you may not be able to break the wools and fill the sail. In this case you must lower the sail to the deck again and break a few open yourself.

Once the sail is stopped up, you must pack it. The best kind of bag is a square one, with the facility to separate the head, tack and clew once

The advantage of the square bag is clear when you come to hook up the sail to the halyard, sheet and the guy. Each corner is clearly marked and separated from the others, making it much simpler to see what attaches to what, and guaranteeing no twists in the sail.

Ready to hoist the spinnaker. The headsail is left hoisted. Use the topping lift and downhaul to set the pole parallel to the deck. Use the guy to pull the tack out to the end of the pole. The guy should be pulled tight against the topping lift and downhaul, and made up on a winch.

(Left) Hoist the spinnaker. It is a good idea, if you have enough crew, for someone to help feed the spinnaker out of the bag. (Right) If you don't pull hard on either the sheet or the guy as the sail is hoisted, you should be able to get to this position, with the spinnaker nicely in the lee of the headsail and still stopped up.

the sail is packed. Feed the sail into the bag from the middle of the foot working towards all three corners at once. Ideally the bag will allow you to velcro or clip the corners apart once the sail is packed. Only then can you be sure that the sail will not go up twisted. If you only have one set of sheets, fit a retrieval line. This is a length of soft, thick rope about six to ten feet long that's attached to the clew. Tie it to the clew after the sail is packed and leave it coiled outside the bag. It gives you something with

which to grab the spinnaker and haul it into the boat when you are lowering it.

The next job is to set up the spinnaker gear. We'll assume that you are using just one set of spinnaker sheets - since we're not planning to gybe the sail. Clear the halyard so that it is outboard of the headsail and clipped to the lifelines near the leeward shroud. Run the leeward sheet from the leeward shroud, outside all the lifelines and rigging, back to the turning

When everyone is ready you can pull the pole and tack aft with the guy, and sheet on at the same time. The wind will start to get into the sail and break the stops, and it will gradually fill.

block and then onto a winch. The windward sheet or guy runs from the leeward shroud forward, round the outside of the headstay, through the outboard end of the pole and back to its turning block and winch. Ensure that it too is outside all the lifelines and rigging. Raise the pole with the topping lift and at the mast, then tighten the downhaul to hold it firmly in place.

Now, with the boat on a broad reach, bring the spinnaker on deck and take it down to the leeward shroud. Clip the sheet to the clew, the guy to the tack (strictly speaking this is called

the forward clew) and the halyard to the head of the sail. Before the halyard goes up pull on the guy until the tack reaches the pole. The headsail should still be up; just ease it a couple of feet from its windward trim, then it won't get in the way of the spinnaker going up. Whenever you hoist a spinnaker that isn't in a sock, do it in the lee of the mainsail and the headsail. The worse thing you can do is hoist it with just the mainsail up on a beam reach. This allows the wind to get into it before you're ready, and that's when the trouble begins.

(Left) Set up ready to drop the spinnaker, on a broad reach with the headsail unfurled. The halyard and guy are ready to run, and someone is to leeward with the retrieval line in his hand, ready to pull. (Right) Ease the guy quickly so that the pole and tack go to the headstay. The spinnaker will start to collapse and the person to leeward starts pulling as hard as he can.

Now we are ready for the perfect hoist. As one person pulls the sail up, it is helpful if another feeds it out of the bag. Don't pull on the sheet (though someone should be holding it) until you've got the sail all the way up. If the sail fills too early everything gets a lot harder. Ideally you've got the head all the way to the masthead, the tack at the end of the pole and the majority of the sail still sitting quietly in the lee of the main and headsail. Now pull the pole and tack aft

together, using the guy, until they are pointing about forty five degrees off the bow. (Remember to ease the downhaul to let the pole come aft.) As you do so the wind will start to get into the sail and break the wool stops. Sheet the sail on at the same time and the spinnaker will start to fill. Once you have the spinnaker filled you can furl the headsail. Grab the retrieval line that is trailing from the leeward clew and tie it off to the guardrail ready for the drop.

Then ease the halyard down as the spinnaker is pulled into the boat. Finally, ease the guy to let the tack into the boat.

Lowering the symmetric spinnaker

The same rule applies for the drop as for the hoist: try and do it on a broad reach, in the lee of the main and headsail. So unfurl the headsail and leave it loosely sheeted. Make sure both the guy and the halyard are free to run, with no knots or loops round the deck gear. Then get someone standing to leeward by the main hatch with the retrieval line (fitted to the leeward clew) in his hand, and get him ready to pull. Let the weather guy go quickly, until the pole gets to the headstay but no further. Do it as fast as you can; that way all the air will go out of the sail and it will disappear round the back of the mainsail and sit there harmlessly. At the same time whoever's on the retrieval line can start pulling in the clew towards them and grabbing the foot of the sail. Ease the halyard down as the spinnaker is pulled into the boat and down the hatch, bunching it together as you do it. Don't let the wind get into the sail and pull it out of your hands. It's only secure when it's down below!

12 Buying sails

However much you pull on the control lines, it won't make much difference to the shape of these sails!

Cruising sails can seem to last forever. It's not uncommon for twenty year old mainsails to be still doing Channel crossings, and the time for new sails is often the moment when the old ones self-destruct in a final blaze of shredded glory, or the sailmaker shakes his head sadly at the winter visit, and says he can't do any more for these... But there are very good reasons for upgrading sails on a more regular basis, not least of which is safety. It's not just a question of changing sails that are going to break - obviously it's dangerous if a sail fails you at a critical moment. But more insidious is the loss of performance that comes with age. Sails that won't hold their shape, and won't drive you upwind off a lee shore with three reefs in, also hold a potential for disaster.

So how do you know when a sail has had its day? A potential breakdown should be visible in the condition of the sail, and we've listed in the next chapter the areas that need attention. The loss of performance is harder to see, particularly in a cruising boat, which doesn't have the competitive performance yardstick of a racer. But perhaps when the sail resolutely refuses your efforts, hopefully inspired by this book, to trim it properly - then it has had enough. When the cloth has broken down and become so stretchy that even in the lightest winds you can no longer apply enough force to the edges or corners to pull it back into shape, then it is time to retire the sail.

Price or performance?

And when you do decide to go for new sails, should you worry about anything other than price? We saw in Chapter 2, for instance, that there are good technical arguments in favour of both bi-radial and tri-radial sails. It is equally clear that they are harder, and therefore more expensive, to manufacture. There are more panels to cut and sew together, and the design is more complex and requires greater sophistication to get the benefits that all that extra work demands. So why bother when cruising sails are not ultimately about performance?

The better the design and the material are, the lighter the sail will be for the same strength. Lighter sails are significantly easier to handle than cumbersome heavy ones. Well designed sails from good quality cloth will invariably last longer than badly designed ones. The loads in the sail will be better matched by the construction, and they will be less likely to distort and break down. Value for money isn't just the lowest price, but is often hiding behind a much longer lifespan. Good sails hold their shape better as they get older, as the wind increases, when they are reefed and furled. And you never know when you are going to need that performance - beating off a lee shore with the engine out or trying to beat a tidal deadline on the bar of a pleasant harbour where you have a restaurant booked.

New sails

So with your cheque book in one hand and a clear conscience in the other, how do you go about buying new sails? Much of the sailmaking process is a balance between conflicting elements; the easiest sail to handle isn't necessarily the longest lasting, the strongest is rarely the lightest and the cheapest isn't always the most cost effective. The correct balance of these factors will be different for every boat owner and their circumstances; not just the type and size of boat and the amount you want to spend - but what kind of sailing do you do and where? How often do you go out? Do you pick your days or go regardless of the weather? Day sailing or blue water cruising? How many

people do you normally sail with? All these elements and others will have an impact on the sail that you should be buying.

The information

The first thing is to gather some details about your boat. If it's a popular One Design then that will probably be enough information for the sailmaker. If not, it will mean taking a few simple measurements so that the sailmaker can give you an accurate quote. They may supply you with a form to fill in with the information they need, or come and measure the boat themselves - though this is more likely to happen once they have the order! But before you contact the sailmaker you should sit down and think about what type of sailing you want to do with your new sails. Then you need to decide what type of sail you think you want, namely: the sail handling system, the sail design, and the construction and cloth type. You could discuss all this with the sailmaker straight away, but it is probably true that the more you know your own mind before you go into the buying process, the more likely you are to get something you will be happy with in the long run. If you change your mind about the sail you want, you will have done so for a good reason.

The sail handling system

Right at the heart of this decision process is the type of sail handling system that you are going to use. Are you going to stick with your present system or change - upgrade to roller reefing maybe, or perhaps go for a cruising chute and launch sock? We have looked at the pros and cons of the various alternatives in Chapter 7, and there is not much that we can add to the discussion here.

Cloth and construction

The precise details of cloth and construction will obviously have a great deal to do with the sailmaker who finally makes the sail. The important thing is that when you are comparing quotes and talking to sailmakers you should know the difference between the cloth types and the designs, which we have discussed in some

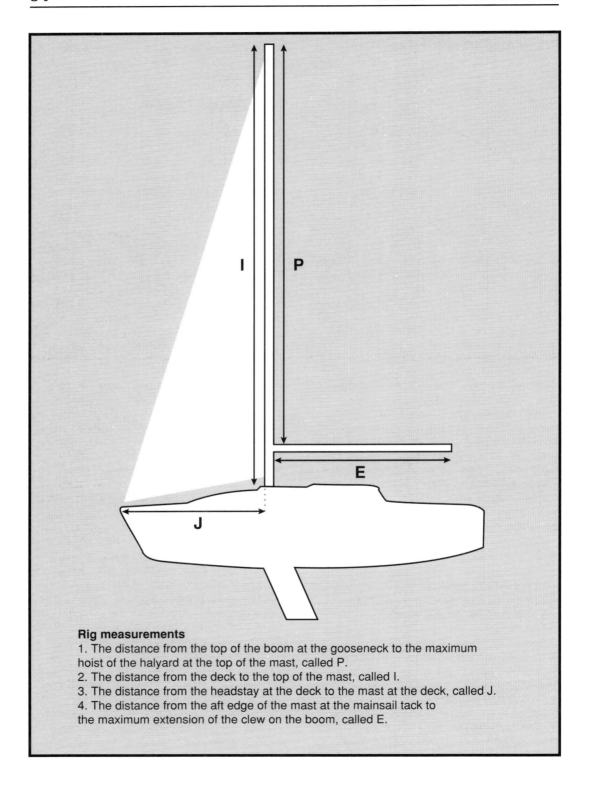

Rig measurements
1. The distance from the top of the boom at the gooseneck to the maximum hoist of the halyard at the top of the mast, called P.
2. The distance from the deck to the top of the mast, called I.
3. The distance from the headstay at the deck to the mast at the deck, called J.
4. The distance from the aft edge of the mast at the mainsail tack to the maximum extension of the clew on the boom, called E.

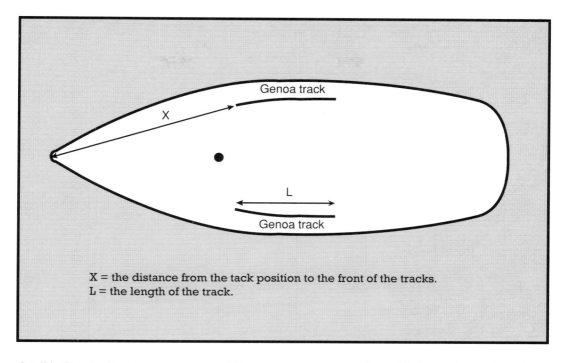

X = the distance from the tack position to the front of the tracks.
L = the length of the track.

detail in Chapter 2. Then you can accurately compare like with like. For instance, there is no point comparing a tri-radial sail from one sailmaker with a cross-cut design from another; the former will always be more expensive. The design and the cloth used in the sail make an enormous difference to its price so make sure you know the design of the sail whose price has been quoted. If the sailmaker is describing the panel layout with a tradename that you don't recognise or understand, ask him to explain whether it is based on a cross-cut, bi-radial or tri-radial layout.

Certainly at some stage you should ask about the type, manufacturer and the weight of the cloth that is being suggested. If anything other than woven polyester is being used you should want to know why - and see some pretty convincing reasoning. There are several major cloth manufacturers who advertise in the yachting press; if you don't recognise the name of the maker of the cloth, ask for the price again with cloth from a manufacturer you have heard of – Contender or Dimension Polyant for instance. Cloth weight is the final hurdle as the different units can be confusing. Grams per

square metre is straightforward enough, and ounces per square yard ought to be – except that in America they use ounces per sailmaker's yard, which is a piece of cloth 28.5 inches wide by 36 inches long! So you need to know if the number is metric, imperial or American. And sometimes the brand name of the cloth will contain a weight that bears no relation to the actual cloth weight under any of these systems!

It is also worth asking what comes with the sail. Are there any bags, and if so, are they big enough to be of any use? This is particularly important with headsails that must be carried on deck and hooked up to the headstay, and spinnakers that must be launched from the bag. The longer and bigger the headsail bag the better, and it should have a full length zip. We've already talked about spinnaker launch bags in Chapter 11. Ask about boom covers to protect mainsails, and about sacrificial sunstrips for roller furling headsails. It is these extras that sailmakers are often most willing to negotiate on to get the order. And if you really want to get a good deal, buy in the Autumn – the sailmaker's traditionally quiet time.

This is an example of the type of form the sailmaker might supply to get the necessary information for a quote or sail construction.

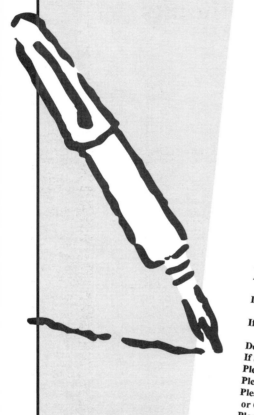

SAIL QUESTIONNAIRE

Please complete the following:-

Rig Type....Masthead ⅞ Rig Fractional (Please delete as necessary)

Does mast bend? If yes please give approximate amount in normal sailing mode at

¼, ½ and ¾ height of luff from tack

¼ .... ½ .... ¾ ....

Backstay Crane - distance from aft face of mast to pin position ....
Approximate height of backstay crane above top of mainsail ....

MAINSAIL

Name of Mast Maker (if known) ....
Model or No: of Mast (if known) ....
Name of Boom Maker (if known) ....
Model or No: of Boom (if known) ....
Are Slides or Boltrope required on (a) Mast ....
(b) Boom ....
If Slides, give Model and Make on (a) Mast ....
(b) Boom ....
If Boltrope, please give diameter on (a) Mast ....
(b) Boom ....
Does Boom have integral Clew Slider ....
If Slides required but not marked, please give drawing showing principal sizes. if yes give details ....
Please confirm Luff length (P) ....
Please confirm Foot length (E) ....
Please confirm Leech length ....
or Give angle between Mast and Boom ....
Please give distance between end of Boom extended to Backstay ....
Are Rows of Slab Reefs required If yes how many ....
Is Sail Insignia required If yes please supply details ....
Are Sail Numbers required If yes please give number ....
Colour of Insignia Colour of Sail Numbers ....

Please complete attached form for Tack Off details.

Is Mainsail to be supplied Cross-cut or Radial Cut ....

Which specification? Cruising Racing Blue Water Cruising
(Please delete as necessary)

Tack offset, tack, reef hooks

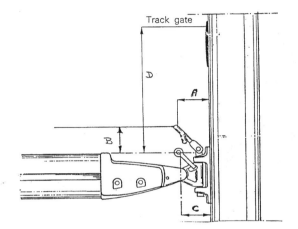

Track gate

Measurements

A., ...

B. ....

C. ....

D. ....

If tack attachment point is above boom line please give distance. ....
Please also give distance between tack pin position and boom entry. ....

SAIL QUESTIONNAIRE

GENOA - FORESAIL

Confirm "I" Measurement ....

Confirm "J" Measurement ....

Is Headsail to be fitted to a Furling Unit ....

If YES, give make of Unit ....

Give maximum Luff length of Sail including Shackles and Tapes ....

Height of Tack of Sail above Deck Line ....

Sail Entry Height above Tack Position ....

Is an Ultra Violet Sunstrip required ....

Which side of Sail is UV Sunstrip to be fitted ....

Is a Foam Insert required in Luff ....

If not does Sail require a Rope or Wire Luff ....

Are Forestay Hanks required .... Diameter of Forestay ....

Distance from Tack position to Front of Tracks ....

Length of Tracks ....

Are Tracks on or above Deck ....

If above give Height ....

Height above Deck Clew required ....

13 Care and repair

The blue strip on the edge of the headsail is the sacrificial sunstrip. It's the only part of the sail exposed to the sun's damaging rays once the sail is furled.

A spreader patch, added to the sail to strengthen it against the inevitable chafing. The spreader end itself should also be taped and smooth.

Sail care

There are six things that will shorten the life of your sails: sunlight, handling, flogging, salt water, chafe and dirt. Sail care means working to avoid this damage - while you are sailing, when you get back from a cruise or day-sail, and at the end of your sailing season before the lay-up period. We will look at each of these in turn.

On the water

While you are out on the water there is obviously a limit to how much care you can take of a sail. It is there to be used, after all. One example is sunlight, which degrades all sailcloth, and while you can't do much about it when the sail is set, there is a lot to be said for covering them when they are not being used. A boom cover and a sacrificial sunstrip on the leech of the furling genoa are an excellent investment in sail longevity. Similarly, if you are motoring in a calm with the main up, it's not a bad idea to take it down and get the boom cover on.

Flogging sails is probably the fastest way to wear them out. The resin finish breaks down and the cloth becomes weaker and stretchier. With modern sail handling technology you should be able to avoid flogging sails except in an emergency. But if you partially furl a headsail and don't move the lead forward, the loose leech can vibrate badly. Equally, if you use sails above the wind strength for which they were designed you may stretch the cloth beyond what is called the yield point - so they will no longer return to their original shape. The use of roller furlers means that most sails are now designed to go right through the wind range, but it is still true that good sail trim will help your sails last longer.

Avoiding chafe requires a little preparation before you start sailing. It's a good idea to go over the boat carefully with a roll of tape and make sure there are no sharp or rough surfaces, pins or screw heads anywhere that the sail can come into contact with (or anywhere at all if you value your oilskins and your health!). The sailmaker should also have patched the sail where the spreaders and the stanchions chafe. The batten pockets on fully battened mainsails are particularly vulnerable to chafing on the shrouds and they must be reinforced by the sailmaker in these areas.

During the season

At the end of any sail, be it a three-week cruise or a day-sail, you have to decide how to store your sails until the next time. We are lucky that modern materials are resistant to moisture and salt crystals, and they can be left on the boat for the duration of the season without incurring unnecessary wear and tear. But if you do have the opportunity to rinse them in this period you should always take it. Salt holds moisture into the cloth, and the crystals will chafe the fibres. Sails made from any cloth are best rolled, as this does less damage to the cloth finish than the creasing that is inevitably involved in folding or

flaking sails. Roller furler systems have this advantage, although it does mean the sail is left to the battering of the elements while it is up there, particularly sunlight. That's the importance of the sunstrip. If you leave the sail on the furler make sure you ease the halyard tension, otherwise you can permanently stretch the sail. If you take your sails off the spars, roll them if at all possible, and get bags big enough that they don't need any further folding. If they are stored down below, politely ask your crew and guests to avoid sitting or standing on them as much as possible!

The one sailcloth material that is badly affected by moisture is nylon; it loses strength and changes shape when wet. Because sails take longer to dry when salty, the best treatment for a nylon spinnaker is to take it home each time and rinse and dry it on the drive or lawn. Alternatively, leaving the sail loose out of the bag in the forepeak is the next best thing. Don't hang sails in the rigging to dry them unless it is completely calm - the flogging does more damage than leaving them wet! Incidentally, none of the materials likes excessive heat, so avoid leaving them in a car in the middle of summer.

At the end of the year

Although sails can mostly be left to their own devices during the summer season, it is well worth storing them properly for the winter lay-up, as even hard wearing modern materials will not take kindly to being left damp, salty, dirty and creased for six months. The main rules are to rinse and dry the sails, then leave them loosely rolled. Wash them if possible - some dirt, like rust, can be corrosive. Once clean store them somewhere dry, cool and out of the sun. Many sailmakers now offer a winter sail valet service that will take all these jobs off your hands. In addition they will check for routine maintenance, much as I will outline in the following section, and do any necessary repairs.

Maintenance

At the end of any season's sailing you should

Either flaking or rolling the sail into a full length bag is a good way to store it - though rolling is the best method, avoiding the creases visible in the photograph.

have a good look at your sails to see if there are any areas that need work. And it's a good idea to do the same check before a period of extended cruising, particularly if you will be some distance from the services of a sailmaker. The luff and foot tapes and bolt ropes are a good place to start. Chafing is the biggest problem, particularly if it has worn right through the cloth to the rope. It can then catch in the groove as the sail is hoisted and tear badly. If you have slides, hanks or cars, have a good look at each of them to see if there is any cracking or signs of fatigue failure (discolouration or roughening of the surface). The attachment of any hardware to the sail is a potential problem area, because of the fastening of soft sailcloth to harder metal and plastic. The headboard, batten pockets and battens, cunningham and outhaul rings are all worthy of careful inspection for chafe and broken stitching. In fact all the seams are worth scanning to see if they are coming apart. Also have a look at the general condition of the cloth, particularly in areas that are prone to chafe on spreaders and stanchions. How soft and pliable is the cloth compared to when it was new? Sail-cloth can be a bit like the brakes on your car - you don't realise how bad it's getting until it's too late.

A typical sail repair kit.

An annual winter service visit to your sail loft is never a bad idea.

Sail repair

Whether you are repairing broken sails or doing preventative maintenance, the principles of sail work are the same. You will need to get some tools together; scissors, palm, needles of various sizes, hot knife (preferably gas or battery operated) and a seam ripper are all relatively specialist to sail repair. More general tools that could be handy and are probably already on the boat include: a hammer, pliers, punch, screwdrivers and a wire cutter. Depending on your sails it is also worth having some spare hardware around, such as the stainless rings for the tack and clew of all the sails, spare sliders and hanks and even the headboard and a set of spare battens if you are really thorough. Pay a visit to the sailmaker and try and get some off-cuts of spare cloth to match each of your sails, a length of nylon webbing and luff tape, sticky-backed Dacron and nylon, and some thread. Once you've got all this together, pack it in a

bag and keep it on board. Whether you are at sea or at home the following are general rules for any sail repair you undertake.

1. Wash the area thoroughly with fresh water and dry it; any sticky backed cloth will fasten better to a clean, dry surface. Remove old stitching from a damaged seam at the same time.

2. Try and find a flat area to work, be it the saloon table or the dining room table. Sticky-backed cloth goes down much more evenly on a flat surface.

3. Don't use a bigger needle than you have to; large holes in light cloth will weaken it.

4. Sticky-backed nylon is often enough to hold a small tear (a couple of inches) together in a spinnaker. Sewing round it is not just a waste of time, the holes may actually make it weaker. Try not to over-do a repair; have a look at what was holding it together before and use that as a guide.

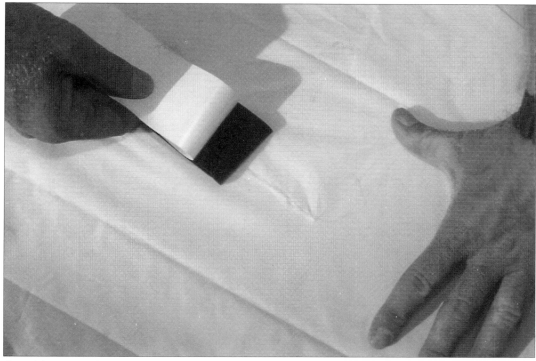

Repairing a tear in a spinnaker with sticky-back tape. This is the type of sail repair job that can be easily tackled at home or on board.

5. When you cut out any sticky-backed cloth to repair a tear, make it about four or five times the diameter of a hole, or six inches longer than a tear and three or four inches wide. Trim any sharp corners so that they are rounded - it makes the fabric much less likely to peel off.

6. Don't peel all the backing off sticky-back cloth at once, lay the whole of one edge first, then peel the backing away as you lay it flat. Smooth it out with your hand, working from the middle towards the edges.

7. If you are replacing hardware, such as broken hanks or slides, have a good look at how the sailmaker did the original job on one that is still fully attached, and copy the technique as far as possible. One tip is to try and pull any webbing tight as you sew it down. Any slackness will be taken up when the load comes on and will allow the repair to work and chafe.

What to fix?

If you're at sea and desperately need to get a sail back into action you won't have much choice but to have a go at fixing it yourself. Mostly sail repair is just common sense, and at sea you won't have to worry about whether or not you need a sewing machine. But it's a different matter when you're at home - should you press the family sewing machine into service to have a crack at getting that clew patch back together? Probably not, unless it's a spinnaker. More than one or two layers of headsail or mainsail sailcloth is more than a match for most non-commercial sewing machines. And if you stick to hand sewing that will give you a pretty good idea of what you can try and fix yourself. When the repair involves ten metres of hand seam sewing, it's trying to tell you to take it to the sailmaker.

A rip or tear in a single panel should be no problem to fix. Once it has crossed a couple of

But even the sailmaker is going to struggle to put this one back together again!

seams it has become more structural and is worth showing to a sailmaker. The same is true of the hardware; hanks and slides away from the corners don't carry much load and you should be able to replace them yourself. But those at the corners do a lot more work and you should be more wary of them. The same goes with clew, tack and head rings. They are all high load areas and not good choices for your first attempt at sailmaking. Conversely, batten pockets are away from the corners and well worth doing yourself.

Are you after Cruising Sails, or some triangles with holes in the corners?

Rick Tomlinson.

Some 'cruising sails' are just that - triangles with holes in the corners. Slabs of cheap cloth, cut and sewn up with a minimum of effort, for a minimum price.

But it can be very different.

At Hyde we have thirty years of experience, winning in the white heat of the world's most competitive racing fleets. We know how sails work. And we apply that technology rigorously to make cruising sails that will handle better, be more efficient and give longer service than anything that has gone before.

These sails are more than just triangles with holes in the corners. These are sails built to perform. These are sails built to last. Hyde Sails.

So if you want Cruising Sails, start by calling Hyde, today.

hyde sails

Main Office. Richard Franks. Tel: 01621 782108.
South Coast Office. Christian Brewer. Tel: 01590 673637
South Coast Agent. Chris Holman Rigging. Tel: 01243 514000.
South West Agent. Mike McNamara. Tel: 01395 264907.
The Sail Loft, Burnham-on-Crouch, Essex CM0 8TB, England.
Fax: 01621 782669. E-mail: TheSalesTeam@HydeSails.co.uk.
Web: http://hydesails.com.

ree technical brochures
ur series of technical brochures
xplains everything you need to know

before you choose a sail – as recommended by Yachts & Yachting. Call 01621 782108 now and we'll send you a free copy.

For once 'Discount' doesn't mean cheap

It's easy enough to get a discount on
triangles with holes in them.
But after reading *'Sails for Cruising
- Trim to Perfection'* we know your
expectations will be higher.
And at Hyde, we like to fulfil
people's expectations.
So here it is -
Hyde Sails with a ten percent discount.
Present this page (or a copy of it)
and Hyde will give you ten percent
off your sail order.
Can we do more than that?
Hyde Sails - this time, you can
get the best for less.

hyde sails

Main Office. Richard Franks. Tel: 01621 782108.
South Coast Office. Christian Brewer. Tel: 01590 673637
South Coast Agent. Chris Holman Rigging. Tel: 01243 514000.
South West Agent. Mike McNamara. Tel: 01395 264907.
The Sail Loft, Burnham-on-Crouch, Essex CM0 8TB, England.
Fax: 01621 782669. E-mail: TheSalesTeam@HydeSails.co.uk.
Web: http://hydesails.com.